The Creative Real Estate Marketing Equation
Motivated Sellers + Motivated Buyers =$

By Omar Johnson

This book is dedicated to my daughter Jelania and my wife Yolanda.

Copyright Notices

Table of Contents

Introduction..7

What are some of the circumstances that make owners of real-estate motivated sellers?..................................8

Your Motivated Seller Marketing System...........................10

50 Secret Insider Techniques and Places You Can Use to Start Finding Motivated Sellers Deals Immediately................13

Finding Motivated Sellers: SEARCHING ON THE GROUND..16

Technique #1: FSBOs 17

Technique #2: Properties for Rent 18

Technique #3: Abandoned Properties 19

Technique # 4: Neighborhood Bulletin Boards 20

Technique #5: Door Fliers 21

Technique #6: Door Knocking........................... 22

Technique #7: Garage Sales.............................. 23

Technique #8: Estate Sales................................ 25

Technique #9: Car Signs 26

Technique #10: Bandit Signs 27

Technique #11: Bird Dogs 28

Technique #12: Mail Carrier............................. 29

Technique #13: Trash Collector 30

Finding Motivated Sellers: Networking Strategies........31

Technique #14: Referrals 32

Technique #15: Other Investors 34

Technique #16: Wholesalers 35

Technique #17: Builders 36

Technique #18: Real Estate Agents 37

Technique #19: Real Estate Attorneys 39

Technique #20: Title Companies 40

Technique #21: Real Estate Inspectors 41

Technique #22: Contractors 42

Technique #23: REI Clubs 43

Technique #24: Community Events 45

Find Motivated Sellers: List Based Techniques...........46

Technique #25: For Sale Ads 47

Technique #26: For Rent Ads 48

Technique #27: MLS 50

Technique #28: Notice of Default List 51

Technique #29: Probate Court 52

Technique #30: Housing Court 54

Technique #31: Bankruptcy Court 55

Technique #32: Code Violation Office 56

Technique #33: Bank REO Departments 57

Technique #34: Fire-Damaged Homes 59

Technique #35: Absentee Owners 60

Technique #36: Aged FSBOs 61

Technique #37: Section 8 Landlord List 62

Finding Motivated Sellers: Places To Advertise...........63

Technique #38: Newspaper Classifieds 64

Technique #39: Online Classifieds 65

Technique #40: Radio Ads 66

Technique #41: Television Ads 67

Technique #42: Outdoor Advertising 68

Technique #43: Telephone Book Ads 69

Technique #44: Direct Mail 70

Technique #45: Magazines 71

Technique #46: Neighborhood Publications.................... 73

Finding Motivated Sellers: The Internet......................74

Technique #47: Lead Generating Services..................... 75

Technique #48: Social Networking Sites........................ 76

Technique #49: Website 77

Technique #50: Tax Deeds 78

Scripts for Your Motivated Seller Prospects...................80

Pre-screen Sellers Script...83

What To Say To An Executor Of An Estate In Probate........85

Motivated Buyers...86

Creating Your Killer Buyers List.............................87

The Two Types of Buyers In The Real Estate Market........89

Prospecting And Marketing: Adding Buyers To Your
List...91

Classified Ads..92

Strengthening Your Buyers List...............................94

What To Say To Your Buyers: 3 Stages of The Buying
Process..97

Introduction

Hello, my name is Omar Johnson, real-estate investor, coach and author and welcome to the book "The Creative Real Estate Marketing Equation". In order for you to succeed as a real estate investor, you must understand the following equation:

Motivated Sellers + Motivated Buyers = $ For You. I'm going to say that again: **Motivated Sellers + Motivated Buyers = $.**

In fact, the combination of motivated sellers and motivated buyers can actually make you filthy stinking rich from real estate. Let me explain further. Once you are able to find a motivated seller and come to an agreement with that seller to creatively purchase their house, you need a motivated buyer to either cash you out and take the property off your hands or at least make some type of monthly payment to you that will enable you to create a positive monthly cash flow from that property. Wouldn't you agree?

In fact, it would even make perfect sense for you to have your pre-screened list of buyers already in the can before you start acquiring inventory, that way you significantly increase your chances of selling that property or profiting from it immediately. The bottom line is quickly turning properties for fast profits is the name of the game and should be your immediate goal and focus as a real-estate entrepreneur, because if you are not able to generate cash flow quickly and continuously, your real-estate investing career will be over before it even starts.

Sounds a little brutal to you? Oh! Well, that's life. I'm just trying to keep it real with you. You have to eat. Don't you? Well, it takes cash flow to do that. Doesn't it? And I'm not talking about the type of cash flow that will only enable you to eat burger and fries from the dollar menu at McDonald's. I'm talking about filet mignon type of cash flow.

I want you to eat well and live well and have the financial freedom to do as you please. The way that you would obtain that much desired financial freedom through your real-estate business is by mastering that equation that I previously mentioned to you. Motivated Sellers + Motivated Buyers = $.

Let's look at that first part of the equation, **Motivated Sellers**. What is the definition of a motivated seller? A motivated seller is someone that needs to sell. You won half of the battle when you understand that there is a big distinction between someone wanting to sell a property versus someone that needs to sell a property. One is a suspect; the other is a prospect.

Someone who just wants to sell a property is usually expecting a buyer to pay retail prices and if they get it fine. And if they don't, it is no big deal. Now, a motivated seller on the other hand has to get rid of that property by any means necessary. They are looking for a solution to their immediate problem, which is the house that they need to get rid of. And if you, the real-estate investor comes up with a workable solution, their house becomes yours at a bargain price.

What are some of the circumstances that make owners of real-estate motivated sellers?

Job relocation. Millions of families travel to new cities and towns when companies shuffle their employees between different locations. This makes selling real-estate a top priority for the moving family.

Job termination. Although no one likes to think about it, millions of people lose their job, which puts their finances at risk and can often lead to selling real-estate to move to a more economical alternative.

Death in the family. Real-estate may be given to one or several family members by a relative who has passed away. If the family already owns real-estate, then one of the two properties is often sold.

Bankruptcy. When someone is completely down on their luck, often the money invested in their real-estate is the only money that they have access to so they must sell quickly.

Retirement. All the individuals who have used rental properties as a source of income may find it too demanding as they get older and sell their real-estate to put the money into savings.

Maintenance woes. After acquiring several properties and buildings in different areas such as a home in the city, a rental property and a cottage, some people may decide it is too much work to maintain them all and want to sell one of them.

Divorce. People sometimes split up, which changes the economic dynamics of their situation. Instead of there being two people sharing a mortgage, you now have in most cases one sole person paying the entire mortgage. This creates a financial strain on them and puts the real-estate investor in the perfect situation to present the perfect solution called debt relief.

Making a payment on two or more houses. Sometimes people face the dilemma of making mortgage payments on two or more houses. For example, maybe they got transferred to a job in another state and had to purchase a house in that state and was unable to sell their original house in a timely fashion.

Your Motivated Seller Marketing System

The bottom line is you must have a marketing system in place that runs on auto-pilot that will enable you to find and attract an avalanche of motivated sellers and deliver them to you like a doctor delivers babies. So why do you need a marketing system in place that will have your phone ringing off the hook with motivated sellers? The answer is, because motivated sellers are the source for generating profits for your real-estate business. Motivated sellers as a result of the aforementioned circumstances will allow you to buy their houses creatively with very little money and no credit simply because they need a non-conventional solution to their real-estate woes.

When you offer that non-conventional solution to them, their house becomes yours once again at a bargain price, which then puts you in the perfect position to realize profits once you have that motivated buyer in place to cash you out. So do you clearly understand why you must have a marketing system in place to find and attract motivated sellers? For the sake of your real-estate investing career, I hope you've answered that question with a resounding "Yes."

Just think about it for a second. All great businesses run themselves automatically by using a system. Your real-estate business shouldn't be any different if you plan to be truly great and rich at what you do. For example, just look at McDonald's. They have an ultra successful franchise system that serves billions of burgers and fries to people.

Ray Kroc, founder of the McDonald's franchise system, basically took what the McDonald brothers were already doing successfully, selling burgers and fast food and duplicated their system to build an astounding worldwide conglomerate. What was that system? Kroc called it "The McDonald's Method", which was basically a system that explained to the franchisees such things like how much meat to include in a burger, how to cut the fries and how often to clean the restaurant.

In fact, McDonald's system is so fine-tuned today that basically high school kids run it. Similarly, you should have a fine-tuned lead generating system in place in your real-estate business that runs on auto pilot 24/7 that will produce motivated seller leads by the boatload. The majority of real estate investors don't understand that they have to have an automated system in place to find motivated sellers as well as motivated buyers simply because they were never taught this at all, or thoroughly by their favorite "real estate guru". I can absolutely guarantee what they did learn was 100 different ways and techniques to put together deals for Lease Options/Options, Wholesaling, Retailing, Getting the Deed, Owner Financing or how to perform a Short Sale.

That's all fine and dandy, but it all means absolutely nothing if you don't know how to get sellers in front of you so that you can construct and present your offers, get them accepted, turn them over to your motivated buyers and in the process make a boatload of cash. Wouldn't you agree? Conversely, your favorite "real estate guru" in their particular course or seminar didn't exactly reveal to you or show you the ton of ways in which you can locate and find motivated sellers.

I guess it's not their focus or maybe they are just leaving out the good stuff so that they can upsell you to some guerilla marketing bootcamp or something similar for $5,000. I'm all too familiar with that game and you are probably too. To their credit, what they probably did teach was that you should put a WE BUY HOUSES—Any Price, Any Condition, Any Area classified ad in your local newspaper. This is good advice except for two things.

1) There are other real estate investors in your area with the same ad in the same newspaper! In my local newspaper there are four such ads including mine.

2) Your phone barely rings. Don't get me wrong your ad should remain in the newspaper all year around if your budget allows it because you just never know when that motivated seller will decide to call you, but by using this approach alone you will be waiting and waiting......for your phone to ring all the while becoming more and more frustrated and wondering if the Real Estate business is for you.

In addition, the majority of the Real Estate Gurus teach you but in the most simple and basic way that you must mail letters to people with houses, but they hardly ever show you:

Who, What, and Where to target

Where's the best place to get a reliable list

How to craft a formulaic letter

How to match your message with your market

How to create a sequential letter system for finding deals

How to use postcards to bring you an avalanche of motivated sellers

How to systemize the entire process so that your business runs on autopilot

You're probably thinking to yourself "wow that's a whole lot to learn". I'm here to tell you that it is not a lot to learn, but it is imperative that you learn these fundamentals or your real estate investing career will be toast. In essence, what it basically comes down to is this: instead of being a real estate entrepreneur, you must become a marketer of your real estate business. If you are in business, you need to make this shift in your thinking. No business is going to prosper without a lot of customers. Making this shift in thinking about who you are focuses you on the singularly most important and financially rewarding aspect of business--marketing. The money is in marketing the business, not in doing the business.

If you are the impatient type, I know that you probably don't have the time or any interest in creating your own bona-fide motivated seller marketing system from scratch. There's a lot of testing involved in creating your own system. You have to see what works and what doesn't work, then fine tune it before you develop a proven system.

So to save you the time, heartache, blood, sweat and tears and the financial cost associated with this process, I'm going to give you complete access to my ready to use proven system of postcards, free reports, flyers, signs, business cards, and ads that you can personally use to attract motivated sellers. I am also going to give you access to my proprietary **Real Estate Investor Sequential Letter System**, which consists of powerful letters and follow up letters that you can mail to the different niches of motivated sellers.

In this ready to use system which I call **"The Real Estate Investor's Guide To Finding Motivated Sellers"** everything is all done for you, so there is no need for you to create these marketing materials from scratch. Just simply edit them and personalize them with your name then send them out and sit back and watch your phone start ringing off the hook with motivated sellers who are dying to do deals with you. Just visit the link below:

http://www.findingthemotivatedsellers.com

50 Secret Insider Techniques and Places You Can Use to Start Finding Motivated Sellers Deals Immediately

Finding motivated seller deals consistently depends on two factors, and these are the same factors that separate successful investors in general from the rest of the crowd: skills, which are learned and mastered, and systems, which are built and perfected. In other words, using the techniques presented in this book to propel your real estate business to massive profits involves developing certain personal skills, such as being able to recognize a potential deal or a marketing opportunity, as well as building certain systems, such as marketing or referral systems, to bring you fresh new deals on a consistent basis.

Skills apply to processes whose nature is such that they vary somewhat each time they are carried out and which require you to use your judgment. Systems are elements that you put in place when there is little variation in the process to make sure that certain standard procedures are carried out automatically.

By constantly systematizing your efforts, improving your systems, and developing your skills you will constantly improve at what you do. Therefore every technique in this book is presented along with a description of the types of skills and systems needed to implement it. Which techniques you choose and how you implement them will also depend on your budget, so an estimate of the cost of each technique is provided as well to help you plan accordingly.

This section of the book presents 50 insider techniques to find motivated seller real estate deals, but there are plenty more techniques to be discovered, because this is an art that is only limited by your creativity. As Albert Einstein said, "Imagination is more important than knowledge", and so it usually is that the more creative your method for finding deals the better, because fewer other investors are likely to be using it already. So, use what you can of the techniques presented here, but don't stop looking for new ways to find deals.

The more sources of deals you have the better. Consider a classified ad you have running in the newspaper. Would you want that ad to be your sole source of deals? Of course not. But if that ad brought you one solid deal in a year, would it be worth running it in addition to your other deal generating techniques? Probably so.

The more doors you have open for the deals to walk through the more you will find coming into your office. Even if you only end up doing a few deals, having more leads to look at will allow you to be more selective and thus increase your profits. Think of real estate as being like fishing: the more lines you have in the water the more and bigger fish you will catch. So implement as many of these deal-finding techniques as you can and watch your business grow in proportion.

Granted that more sources of deals is better than fewer, this doesn't mean that you should be spending time or money in places that don't produce results. It is important to track where your leads come from and where they go so that you can keep tabs on how effective your marketing is. Carefully tracking your results will allow you to spend the most time and money on the processes that produce the best results, which will in turn maximize your profits.

For each technique that you implement, you should keep a record of how many leads you get from it and how many of them turn into deals, as well as the time or money cost per lead and per deal. Implementing this practice consistently will allow you to optimize your business machine over time to generate the greatest possible profits with the least possible expense.

Keep in mind, though, that this doesn't mean that just because something you try doesn't appear to produce results at first you should give up on it, because persistence is necessary for almost all marketing methods, and even a technique that only produces a few leads per year can still be cost effective. Giving a technique enough time to work is an important element of the recipe for success.

Finding Motivated Sellers: SEARCHING ON THE GROUND

The first place to start looking for motivated seller deals, especially if you are new to investing or just new to the neighborhood, is on the ground. You can find many deals that other investors won't find by just going to an area and looking around. This is called farming the neighborhood.

Being in the neighborhood consistently provides valuable experience and allows you to become intimately familiar with your target market, something that will not only give you an edge in finding and acting on deals but also in negotiating. If you ever have difficulty making an offer to a seller, it is most likely because you are unsure of the value, which is a symptom of being unfamiliar with the location. When you know a neighborhood like the back of your hand you will display no hesitation in making your offer or in backing it up.

Furthermore, looking for deals by going to the neighborhood itself will allow you to find deals that aren't widely advertised and which a techno-junkie investor will never find by scouring internet classifieds or seller lists. Many times you can find deals that aren't even on the market to begin with; several of the techniques presented in this section show various ways this can be done. But basically it's just a matter of contacting the owner and making an offer, whether or not the property has a For Sale sign in front of it.

And finally, spending time in your target neighborhood will allow it to become familiar with you, giving you the opportunity to meet the residents face to face and giving you a true community presence. The more chances people have to see you out doing your job the more they can become familiar with you, thus making them more likely to do business with you than with someone they have never seen or met.

The following several techniques give you methods that you can apply by going directly into the neighborhood to find leads and make your presence known in various ways, which is akin to beating the bushes to rustle up the game.

Technique #1: FSBOs

Skills: spotting leads, talking to sellers

Systems: capturing and tracking leads

Cost: gas money

Any houses you see in your target neighborhood that have "For Sale By Owner" signs are fair game, and you should capture and call all of these types of leads. Homes that look run-down or abandoned can be gems, but so can nicer-looking homes; the house doesn't have to be ugly for the seller to be motivated.

Even if the seller isn't motivated you can at least check on the price and thus add to your knowledge of values in the neighborhood. And, just because the seller isn't motivated now doesn't mean that things won't change down the road that might cause the seller to become motivated in the future (see Aged FSBOs for more on this subject). So you should capture all of the FSBO signs you see in your target neighborhood and call them.

On your initial phone call you should determine the price, determine if the seller is motivated, and let them know who you are and what you do. It's generally good to let them know right up front that you are a professional and even if they don't seem interested leave them with your name and contact info in case they change their minds. It also wouldn't hurt to ask if they have any other properties they want to sell; most won't, but a certain percentage will, and a certain percentage of those will be bargains.

Spotting what you're looking for is a matter of skill, as is talking to sellers to determine motivation or make an offer. If you want to do a lot of deals you have to look at a lot of leads, so you should create or borrow a system for capturing, organizing and tracking these leads efficiently. As long as you have money to drive a car this technique is affordable.

Technique #2: Properties for Rent

Skills: spotting leads, talking to landlords

Systems: capturing and tracking leads

Cost: gas money

In addition to properties that are for sale by owner, you should also capture and call the numbers on signs for any properties you see that are for rent by the owner. This includes single family homes as well as multifamily buildings (duplexes, apartments, etc). The reason is simple; a landlord is someone who owns properties, and therefore might be interested at any given time in buying or selling. So you should call them and ask if they have any properties they are interested in selling.

This is one way to find properties before they are officially on the market; the landlord might not have been thinking about selling, or might not have made the decision to sell, until you called and put the idea in his mind. What's also great about calling landlords is that you can build your list of investor buyers this way as well, which is important to have if you want to incorporate wholesaling as a part of your overall business strategy.

Don't just call these leads and throw them away; you should keep a record of each landlord you talk to and follow up with them periodically to check for new potential deals. Also don't forget to give them your name and contact information and tell them what you do so they can get in touch with you if they need to.

As with FSBOs, staying attentive and spotting what you're looking for is a learnable skill, as is chatting with landlords and collecting the relevant information. Also as with FSBOs you will want to have a systematic process for capturing, organizing, and tracking large numbers of leads as efficiently as possible to maximize your chances for success.

Technique #3: Abandoned Properties

Skills: spotting leads, talking to owners

Systems: capturing, organizing, and tracking leads, skip tracing service

Cost: gas money plus skip tracing service (varies, about$1 to $10 per lead)

While you are in your target neighborhood another type of lead you should be constantly scanning for is abandoned properties. Some neighborhoods have more abandoned properties than others, but most will at least have a few, and following these leads will often take you to a seller who is motivated or who simply doesn't know what to do and could use some help.

Why would somebody abandon a property they own? These properties could be foreclosures of one sort or another; or the owner could have been forced to relocate in a hurry, such as for a new job; or the property might have been inherited by someone who is too busy to take care of it; or the owner may own it free and clear and simply have nothing better to do with it.

The catch is that since these owners aren't advertising, you have to take some extra steps to locate and contact them. Given the property address, the county appraisal district will be able to supply you with the owner's name, and you can hire a professional skip tracing service, like www.findtheseller.com, to provide you with that owner's contact information. Of course you can find these elusive owners yourself if you have the appropriate know-how.

Spotting abandoned properties is a more refined art than spotting FSBO or For Rent signs, and is a skill that can be practiced and improved. So is finding the owners, which may involve talking to neighbors or relatives, as well as talking to them once you contact them. You should take a systematic approach to capturing, organizing, and tracking these leads as well as tracking down the owners. The costs involved are gas money and skip tracing services, which can vary in the neighborhood of $1 to $10 per lead.

Technique # 4: Neighborhood Bulletin Boards

Skills: creating fliers, discovering locations

Systems: printing and distributing fliers, phone system

Cost: cost of printing

You can make the most of your time in the field by spreading your business literature and advertising in your wake. One way to do this is by distributing fliers on various bulletin boards in the neighborhood. These are often found in various local businesses and public locations. If you are spending time in your target area looking for leads and keeping a pulse on the neighborhood, you are likely to spot a variety of locations that will support this type of advertising. If your target neighborhood is the type of area that has laundromats, for example, these are good to note because they almost always have bulletin boards that get seen regularly. Check other businesses and stores as well as government buildings as well.

This type of advertising is both inexpensive and targeted, appearing as it does directly in front of your prospects where they live, so it can get your marketing message in front of people who live in your neighborhood for fairly cheap. Needless to say, the more of these you have, the better. Contacting sellers can get you deals reliably, but it's also important to get phone calls coming in to your office so that prospecting isn't your only source of leads.

The skill set for this technique is fairly simple, specifically creating fliers and discovering locations to post them, but even these simple skills can be refined to some degree. You should have a system in place to print and distribute your fliers, as well as a system for receiving and managing the calls when they come in. The cost associated with this technique is minimal and is just the cost of printing fliers, which is in pennies.

Technique #5: Door Fliers

Skills: creating marketing materials

Systems: printing and distributing fliers, phone system

Cost: cost of printing, distributing

An even more direct way to get your marketing message in front of the people who live in your target neighborhood is to distribute door fliers. These can be in the form of hangers that hang on the doorknob, like Domino's Pizza, or post-it notes that stick on the door, like UPS.

The marketing message is something that can be optimized to your target market; the more the message seems to be coming from a real local individual rather than a faceless corporation the more likely people will be to respond to it. You can saturate a neighborhood with your marketing message this way by blanketing it street by street, but you don't have to do all the labor yourself.

This is a task that can be hired out fairly easily (check the yellow pages for companies that provide this service in your target market), and you can pay per flier distributed. The only real skill involved with this technique is creating the flier, which is something that can certainly be improved with experience. The more compelling of a marketing message you can craft, the better the response rate you will get from your efforts.

You will want to have a system for printing and distributing the fliers door-to-door in the target neighborhood you choose, and also a phone system that will ensure incoming calls are not lost so no potential deals get off the hook. Costs will include printing the fliers as well as distributing them, if you choose to hire it out, but this can still be considered one of the cheaper forms of advertising.

Technique #6: Door Knocking

Skills: personal presentation, talking to homeowners in person

Systems: coordinating visits, tracking leads

Cost: gas money

Knocking on doors and encountering homeowners face to face is about as direct a marketing method as you can get, and like all methods it has its advantages and its drawbacks. One drawback is that it takes a fair amount of time, effort, and drive, but an advantage is that it allows you to make a direct impression and work on the homeowner with the full force of your personal magnetism.

You could canvass an entire neighborhood by going door to door, or you could single out particular houses that look to be the most promising prospects based on whatever buying criteria you have. It takes a lot of guts to implement this technique, but it is cheap and the experience can be valuable; after you land a couple of deals this way you will feel like you have paid your dues.

It should go without saying (but I'll say it any way) that any time you knock on a door you should be prepared with copies of your business card and a clipboard for capturing important information from whomever you speak with.

Besides being able to handle rejection, making a good impression is an important skill for implementing this technique, as is talking to homeowners to determine their motivation level and convince them to do business with you. It is also important to have a system for coordinating your visits so that you can keep your efforts focused and consistent. The only cost associated with this technique is gas money.

Technique #7: Garage Sales

Skills: personal presentation, talking to homeowners in person

Systems: capturing and tracking leads

Cost: gas money

Some of the best ways to find deals are indirect because they allow you to find deals that aren't already on the market. This allows you to be the first investor to make an offer, which is a big negotiating advantage. This technique is one example of such an indirect method.

Suppose you see a garage sale going on while driving in a neighborhood. Why do people have garage sales? Sometimes, but not always, it's because they are moving. If it happens that they are, then they might also have a need to sell their house. So, if you see a garage sale going on and stop and talk to the owner, you just might happen to discover a motivated seller.

If you don't happen to discover a motivated seller, it will at least be worth a few minutes of your time while driving a neighborhood to get to know one of the locals and hand out a copy of your business card. Of course you will want to let them know who you are and what you do, just like any time you talk to somebody new while on the job. If you want to get really creative with this technique why not look for garage sale ads in the classifieds and call any that have phone numbers?

Like all prospecting techniques, this is a numbers game, meaning that you may need to try quite a few in order to get the probability of success on your side, but your personal presentation skills are also a factor. So is your ability to talk to a motivated seller in person once you have found one. Improving these skills will improve how well this technique works. And of course, a good lead is wasted if you don't follow up on it, so you should have systems for capturing and tracking leads in place to prevent this. This technique is virtually free; if you happen to be driving somewhere and spot a garage sale, it doesn't cost anything to pull over.

Technique #8: Estate Sales

Skills: talking to sellers

Systems: capturing and tracking leads

Cost: minimal

Usually when someone passes away the majority of their physical belongings are sold at an estate sale for the benefit of the heirs. Going to an estate sale is a little bit like going to a garage sale, except that literally everything is usually on sale, often even including the house itself.

You might see an estate sale while driving through a neighborhood, or you might find ads for them in the local classifieds. Either way these are leads worth following up on; houses that you find for sale under these circumstances are likely to have motivated sellers. Often the house will be sold by somebody who didn't earn the equity themselves, which puts you at an advantage for negotiating purposes as well, since they are likely to have less experience with the property and be less attached to it than an original owner.

Your skill at talking to these sellers is something that can be improved with experience and practice, which will show itself in the form of better results with this technique. These leads should be captured and followed up with systematically just like any other types of leads, to make sure none slip through the cracks. Finding these leads costs practically no money, unless you drive around looking for them, in which case you have to pay for the gas to do this.

Technique #9: Car Signs

Skills: designing marketing materials

Systems: printing signs, phone system

Cost: less than $200

As long as you're spending a lot of time in your target neighborhood, you might as well have your marketing message visible to as many people as possible. One way to achieve continuous visibility is to put signs on your car. These car signs are magnets or decals that stick, or possibly get painted, on your car doors and ensure that everyone who sees you driving will know who you are and what you do (which is what you want, right?).

This probably won't get people calling you in droves, and it shouldn't be your only form of advertising all by itself, but if you do a lot of driving it will probably be cost effective for the five to ten leads per year you can expect it to bring you. If you have any qualms about looking like a dork using this form of advertising just ask yourself this question: would you rather be cool or would you rather be rich?

Some signs will work better than others, so your skill in designing marketing materials can pay off here and is something that you can work to improve. You will most likely pay for someone else to use their system to print these signs for you, but you should make sure that your phone system is geared to receive and capture any and all calls that come in. You should shop around to find the best price for these signs, which should be under $200 and hopefully won't break your budget.

Technique #10: Bandit Signs

Skills: designing marketing materials, placing signs

Systems: printing signs, phone system

Cost: $100-$300

Bandit signs are usually the second rung up the advertising ladder for real estate investors, and are about the cheapest form of outdoor advertising there is. Bandit signs are simply signs that you stick in the ground, on telephone poles, or in other visible locations around your target area.

Of course they should display your marketing message and contact info, and of course they should be placed near busy intersections or other places where they will be seen by plenty of observers who have the opportunity to capture the information. Be aware, however, that the reason they are called bandit signs is because they are prohibited in some places by neighborhood ordinances; if you offend the locals by means of your flagrant advertising it is unlikely to help your business build a good name.

Once placed, bandit signs often tend to have a short life span, but this can be maximized with proper placement. In case you're worried that your sign won't get noticed because there are so many others, keep in mind that there's a reason they are used so much: they work.

Improving your skill at designing an attractive marketing message and at placing your signs in locations where they will stay up, get noticed, and avoid giving offence will make this technique work better for you. You should have a system for printing the signs as well as for fielding the calls they bring in, lest they go to waste. Bandit signs are pretty cheap individually, generally between $1 and $2 per sign, but the cost multiplies when printing and placing a large number of them (which you will probably want to do).

Technique #11: Bird Dogs

Skills: teamwork, motivating others

Systems: managing bird dogs, tracking leads, processing referral fees

Cost: percentage of profit

When you are just starting out as a new investor, it is often necessary for you to fulfill many roles yourself, and this experience with running all of the facets of the business in minute detail can be quite valuable. But, as you gain experience and your business grows over time, it can become impractical to do everything yourself. Fortunately there are many ways you can work with other people to grow your business. One of these ways is by using bird dogs, which generally means someone who agrees to scout out deals in exchange for a referral fee, or a percentage of the profits when the deal is completed. Bird dogs could be anybody, but they are often beginning real estate investors themselves, trying to gain experience in the field.

A bird dog should be somebody who is willing to work for a referral fee, but motivation may still be a challenge, which is why the better you are at motivating other people the better this technique will work for you. Good teamwork skills will help you stay coordinated with multiple bird dogs and keep things running smoothly.

You should have a systematic way of managing your bird dogs, as this will allow you to scale the system, expanding it to any size you wish. And the more leads you deal with the more important it becomes to have a system for tracking and following up with them. Also very important is a system for processing referral fees to make sure they get paid promptly when the deal is done. More than almost anything else, having a reputation for closing deals and paying referral fees will make networking and word-of-mouth advertising work in your favor.

One advantage of working with bird dogs is that you don't pay them up front; you pay them when you get paid, and so the money doesn't come out of your pocket. A standard referral fee is 10% of your profit from the deal.

Technique #12: Mail Carrier

Skills: personal presentation

Systems: tracking leads, processing referral fees

Cost: percentage of profit

The best bird dogs are present in the neighborhood on a consistent basis and are familiar with the houses, people, and happenings there. So naturally a mail carrier would be a perfect candidate. Think about it: a mail carrier is in the neighborhood on a consistent basis, is personally acquainted with every house and its residents, and automatically knows when a house becomes vacant or goes up for sale. Most of them would probably be happy to have a little extra income for passing on any good leads they come across as well.

Consider the mail carrier to be your best friend and get excited every time you see one. Introduce yourself and your business, and of course have a business card ready that briefly describes your referral program. Instant bird dog!

Don't forget to ask them their name, and be sure to remember it or write it down if you can't trust your memory; it always feels nice when you call someone and they remember your name, and crummy when they don't, so you should be prepared, because this is a person who might call you with a $10,000 deal some day soon. The more mail carriers who have your contact info and know about your referral program, the better.

Improving your personal presentation skills will improve your chances of making this technique work. Charisma and charm go a long way towards convincing people to work with you. Like all leads you will want to be systematic about tracking and following up with ones that come in this way, because any bird dog will lose interest quickly if they can't see that anything is happening with their leads. You will also want a system to ensure that you pay referral fees frequently and promptly so that word of your generous nature will spread around. The only thing this will cost is the standard 10% of your profit once the deal closes, a small price to pay for a reliable source of deals.

Technique #13: Trash Collector

Skills: personal presentation

Systems: tracking leads, processing referral fees

Cost: percentage of profit

Similarly to the mail carrier, the trash collector is in an ideal position to be aware of the comings and goings in a neighborhood and to spot fresh deals as soon as they arise. Due to the nature of their job a trash collector will know which houses are for sale, which are unoccupied, and which houses the occupants have recently moved out of, all valuable sources of leads. And presumably, anyone you meet who gets paid to collect garbage is likely to be interested in earning some extra money (either that or a Zen Buddhist, in which case this probably won't work).

If you look around you will probably find even more types of employees whose jobs have them outside in the neighborhood consistently; the more time you spend in your target neighborhood yourself, the more likely you are to run into them.

For example, there are utility company employees, city or county employees, code inspectors, and delivery drivers for UPS or FedEx. What about the person who gets paid to hang door advertisements (ala technique # 5), or the people who go door to door to evangelize or to sell something, or the pizza delivery driver, or the pet and plant sitter, or the lawn service employee? All of these types can potentially be enlisted in your bird dog army, to be your eyes and ears on the ground and bring you leads before anybody else becomes aware of them.

Any time you are enlisting the cooperation of another person you are more likely to have a successful outcome the better your personal presentation skills are, so these are something you should always be seeking to improve. It is as important to have a system to track and consistently follow up with these leads as any others, and also to process referral fees so you can be sure they get paid regularly and promptly. Referral fees are critical to keep up with, because whether you do pay them or whether you don't, either way word gets around fast. The only thing this source of leads will cost you is the standard 10% referral fee, or whatever you negotiate.

Finding Motivated Sellers: Networking Strategies

Most likely your goal as a real estate investor is not to spend the rest of your career driving neighborhoods to look for deals. To accelerate your business into high gear you will ultimately need to have leads coming to you regularly and passively. The best way to do this long term is through networking, which means reaching out to other people who have the potential to send you leads and providing them with an incentive to do so.

One form of incentive you can use to get people to send you deals is monetary; you can offer a referral fee to anyone who will send you a lead that turns into a deal. Another one, which is perhaps even more powerful, is reciprocation. This means doing unto others as you would like them to do unto you.

This is how reciprocation works: There are many other types of real estate professionals that you will encounter in the course of doing business. All of these professionals have access at times to buyers or sellers who could benefit from being referred to you. They also have their own particular type of client that they look for. You can initiate reciprocation by sending them a lead that is no good to you but that might be valuable to them.

For example, if you come across a buyer who is looking for a mortgage to purchase a house you can refer that buyer to a mortgage broker in your network; that makes it likely that the next time that mortgage broker comes across a motivated seller or a buyer who needs a house, you will be the one that gets the referral. It's as simple as that.

Networking works both ways; the more leads you send out into your network the more you are likely to get back; the more value you provide for members of your network, the more value you are likely to receive. If you become a master of networking, the most valuable asset you possess will be your Rolodex. The next several techniques presented all have to do with getting the right people to know about you and your business in order to get the referral pipeline flowing in your direction.

Technique #14: Referrals

Skills: personal presentation

Systems: tracking leads, processing referral fees

Cost: percentage of profit

This is like having the entire world be your bird dog. Implement a referral program and advertise it widely: let the whole world know that you will pay a 10% finder's fee to anybody who sends you a lead that you are able to close. Include this message while talking, in your marketing materials, and certainly on your business cards.

Business cards are particularly relevant to this type of marketing, and you should distribute them at every opportunity: to every person you meet; to friends, relatives, and complete strangers; at gatherings and in public places; in waiting rooms, offices, and businesses; in every piece of mail that leaves your home or office, including utility payments. You can even double up and give people two, encouraging them to give one away. The effect of a single business card released into the wild is small but cumulative; the more of them you have in circulation, the more leads will be able to find their way into your office.

When networking it is important not only that people know who you are when they meet you, but that they remember you. Sharpening your personal presentation skills will help you to gain favor with new people you meet, and will also help you to make a lasting impression so that they will think of you at the appropriate time and remember your referral program.

As with bird dogs it is important to have systematic ways to stay on top of your leads so that you are doing deals and paying referral fees regularly. Receiving a referral fee just for providing a lead tends to do wonders for people's enthusiasm, and few people can keep quiet about a good thing. The cost of implementing this method won't come out of your pocket but will merely be 10% of your profits. Wouldn't you be happy to sacrifice $1,000 to earn $9,000 and be sure of having more leads coming in?

Technique #15: Other Investors

Skills: personal presentation, negotiation

Systems: tracking leads

Cost: highly variable

Many people think of business in general, especially real estate, as being highly competitive, but this is small minded. You are better off thinking of everyone in the real estate business as a potential partner. This should be obvious once you realize three things. The first is that there are many different types of leads, and each investor usually has a specialty. The second is that there are nearly as many ways to do deals as there are investors, so any lead can almost always be worked in multiple ways. The third is that no matter what market you happen to be in there are almost certainly more deals that don't get done than deals that do and new ones are arising all the time, so the supply of deals is virtually unlimited.

You will get much more benefit from seeking ways to cooperate with other investors so that everyone can do as many deals as possible than from trying to steer clear of them as competition. Think of real estate as being like a game where the objective is for all players to get as many deals done as possible. You should talk to other investors whenever possible and inform them of your referral program.

Here are just a few scenarios for how this networking with other investors could be to your advantage. Another investor might receive a type of lead that they aren't able to work with and you are – referral. Or another investor might receive a lead that is outside of their target market and inside of yours – referral. Or the other investor might have a lead that they are just too busy to follow up on but don't want to go to waste – referral. Hopefully you are starting to see the picture – cooperation makes it happen.

The better your personal presentation skills the better the results you can get from cooperating with other investors, and since you are dealing with professional negotiators, any improvement to your negotiation skills is likely to pay off as well. As always you need to be systematic about tracking and following up with these leads and about paying referral fees so that your solid reputation for reliability will precede you. The costs of cooperation are likely to be no more than the standard referral fee and a little reciprocation.

Technique #16: Wholesalers

Skills: personal presentation, negotiation

Systems: tracking leads, processing referral fees

Cost: highly variable

If you are an investor looking for deals wholesalers can be valuable contacts to have in your network. Wholesalers specialize in selling properties to investors, so they can provide you with pre-packaged deals and save you a lot of trouble. Whatever type of deal you are looking for, it is likely that there is a wholesaler who sells them. And if you are a wholesaler yourself, other wholesalers are still valuable for you to connect with for all of the reasons listed in technique # 15, above.

Wholesalers are connectors of people and tend to be very active in the investment community, since their role depends on having many sources of deals as well as many sources of investor buyers. They tend to know a lot of people, and if they can't help you with something real estate-wise they are likely to know someone who can.

If you ever need access to a certain type of real estate professional you can usually ask a wholesaler for a referral and they will be glad to give it – by doing so you will actually be helping them to build good will with someone in their network. Likewise, send a wholesaler a lead that they can work with and you become likely to receive one in return. So connect with wholesalers whenever you can, let them know who you are and what you do, and reserve a special section of your Rolodex for them.

Your personal presentation and negotiation skills will help you get the most benefit from your interactions with wholesalers, although they tend to be helpful regardless, so your results with this technique will improve as you strengthen these fundamental skills.

Efficient, loss-proof systems for tracking leads and for processing referral fees are important for the success of this technique as well. If you actually buy a deal from a wholesaler there is no conventional amount that you can expect to pay; wholesalers negotiate whatever assignment fee they can make room for into the cost of the deal.

Technique #17: Builders

Skills: negotiation

Systems: finding and tracking leads

Cost: minimal

Builders like to build. They like to build so much that sometimes they build more houses than they can sell quickly, resulting in a surplus of inventory. Builders are often highly dependent upon financing and operate with thin margins, so when they acquire a surplus of inventory it tends to put the squeeze on them and they become motivated sellers. When a builder needs to liquidate excess inventory, you would like to be the first one that they call, wouldn't you? That's why it is good to have builders in your network.

Overbuilding is actually quite a common phenomenon and can result in you acquiring brand new properties at a substantial discount. And, like all real estate professionals, builders also occasionally encounter the types of leads you're looking for, and for those instances you want to make sure that they know about your referral program. Implementing this technique is as easy as compiling a list of builders in your target area and calling them to let them know who you are, what you do, and what you're looking for.

Even motivated builders are likely to be skilled negotiators, so as your negotiation skills improve you will likely find that this technique works better and better for you. While there are plenty of builders around, they tend not to advertise very broadly, so a systematic method of finding these types of leads will serve you well, as will a system for tracking and following up with them to prevent any jumping off the hook. There are no specific costs associated with this technique other than the regular costs associated with running a business.

Technique #18: Real Estate Agents

Skills: scouting talent

Systems: tracking leads

Cost: commission

A competent and efficient real estate agent can be a valuable member of your network as well as a good source of deals, while an incompetent one will just waste your time. Keep in mind that real estate agents are a dime a dozen, but the ones that can truly be an asset to you as an investor are relatively rare, so you can afford to be selective about which ones you work with.

Basically, it's a real estate agent's job to sign a buyer's agent agreement with you and get you to buy properties, earning a commission on each one. They have access to the multiple listing service, or MLS (see technique # 27), a directory of properties for sale which is generally only accessible to licensed real estate agents.

A real estate agent can not only bring you leads but also screen them for you. A good real estate agent will apply your buying criteria just as meticulously as you would, so that you look at nothing except for high quality deals. More than just a trumped-up bird dog, however, a good real estate agent will handle negotiating on your behalf and coordinate the entire transaction so that it runs smoothly, handling all of the necessary paperwork from contract to closing, including arranging for any financing that might be involved. If you prefer and can afford a hands-off approach to investing, a good real estate agent can be invaluable to you.

There is very little skill necessary to work with a real estate agent, other than the ability to select a good one, but even this is something that can be improved with experience. If selected well the agent will handle most of the details for you, but you should still have a system in place for keeping up with your own leads. A real estate agent will charge a commission for completing a transaction, which is a percentage of the purchase or sale price. The standard industry figure is 6%, but this is not fixed and can vary based on individual circumstances and negotiation.

Technique #19: Real Estate Attorneys

Skills: personal presentation, phone skills

Systems: tracking leads

Cost: referral fee

Real estate attorneys can be valuable members of your network as well as important sources of deals for your real estate business. This is because they typically encounter all types of real estate situations, including motivated sellers, but they are usually not investors themselves. They help people in all sorts of situations from litigation to probate, and often a fast sale of a property for cash is just what their clients are in need of. In many cases you will actually be doing them and their clients a favor by helping them dispose of unwanted assets.

When you introduce yourself to a real estate attorney you should let them know who you are and what you do, of course, including your referral program, and also find out what their area of specialty is, so that you can refer appropriate clients to them whenever you have the opportunity. The better you are at making a positive impression the more success you will be able to have with this technique, so your personal presentation skills are important.

You are likely to be contacting the attorney's office by phone, so the more skilled you are at communicating over the phone the better off you will be. You should be systematic about tracking and following up with these leads, like always, of course. One advantage of using this technique is that it's practically free, except of course for the regular costs of doing business (such as running an office) and any referral fees that you agree to pay.

Technique #20: Title Companies

Skills: personal presentation, phone skills

Systems: tracking leads

Cost: referral fees

In some states the closing of real estate transactions is handled by real estate attorneys' offices, and in some it is handled by dedicated closing companies, called title companies. If you live in a title company state then these locations will be fairly easy to find. There will be local companies as well as national ones that have many branches.

Trust is the main issue to keep in mind when dealing with title companies; it is important that you come across to them as being professional and serious about what you do. Title companies encounter more than their share of novices and time wasters, and you don't want to be labeled as either; they have a strong preference for working with people who have a reputation for getting deals done.

The best way to introduce yourself to a title company is with a referral; whenever possible you should try to speak to a specific person at the title company and let them know who you got their name and contact info from. In this part of the business relationships are especially important, so a title company that you have used before is the best one to approach.

Whenever you close a deal, be sure to let your title agent know about your referral program and the types of deals you are looking for. Title agents, like real estate attorneys, encounter all types of situations on a regular basis, including those where a fast sale is necessary, and they are always looking for ways to bring more business. For example, a title agent may have an open file where the seller is ready to sell but the buyer backs out at the last minute and leaves everyone hanging. Or a would-be buyer might need to close on the sale of one property before buying another. Ideally you will be the professional buyer who receives the call when these types of situations arise.

Your ability to present yourself professionally, whether in person or over the phone, is an important skill for enlisting the help of title companies to find deals. The better you are able to become at this the more luck you will have with this technique. As with any leads you come across, it is important to use a systematic approach to tracking these and following up with them; a reputation for sloppiness will not help you gain the good favor of any title company.

This technique costs nothing to implement, except possibly for any referral fees you agree to pay, but even this may not be necessary in all cases since title companies are likely to be interested in getting deals done with or without this extra incentive.

Technique #21: Real Estate Inspectors

Skills: personal presentation, phone skills

Systems: tracking leads

Cost: referral fee

In real estate, inspectors are responsible for inspecting the structure and systems of a property and providing their clients with a report detailing any faults that the property may have. They are hired by buyers to inspect properties before they buy them as well as by sellers for the purposes of achieving a faster sale. So, like all real estate professionals, they encounter all sorts of situations on a regular basis, making them worthy of including in your referral network.

Real estate inspectors should be included in your Rolodex for those occasions when you might need their services or when you might be able to do someone else a favor by referring them to a real estate inspector that you know. Of course any time you talk to a real estate inspector you should let them know who you are, what you do, and inform them of the details of your referral program. In addition to meeting lots of sellers and buyers, real estate inspectors generally spend much of their working time in the field, giving them the potential to be effective bird dogs if properly inclined and motivated.

As with all networking methods, your skills at making a favorable impression in person or over the phone are what will make this technique work for you, so these are skills that you should be constantly looking to improve. Also as with other networking methods, you will want to have a system for tracking the leads you receive this way to ensure that each and every one gets the proper amount of attention. Talking to inspectors generally costs nothing, so your standard referral fee is generally the only cost associated with implementing this technique.

Technique #22: Contractors

Skills: personal presentation, phone skills

Systems: tracking leads

Cost: referral fee

Contractors are in the construction business, and they get paid to do everything from new construction to remodeling to minor repairs. They are rarely involved in the buying or selling process, but they are an important ingredient to have in your referral network even if you don't use them in your own business because they are in high demand with investors generally, and you never know when you might be able to gain favor by giving away a referral for a reliable contractor.

Like real estate agents, contractors are plentiful, but unreliable ones are much easier to find than good ones, so you should seek to connect with those who have strong reputations and who come highly recommended by other investors. Like inspectors, their job has them in the field often, making them ideally positioned to act for you as bird dogs if properly incentivized.

If you hire contractors to work for you, you can have them fill out a report to provide detailed information about each property they visit, including any other vacancies or properties for sale on the street, thus adding to your supply of incoming leads. To make this technique work for you, you should talk to as many contractors as possible and let each one know who you are and what you do, with particular emphasis on your referral program.

Your personal presentation skills, both on the phone and in person, are important for making networking techniques work in general, and that is true of using contractors to help find leads as well. Being organized and systematic in tracking and following up with leads you receive this way is also good both for your business and for your reputation. It doesn't cost anything to locate contractors or to talk to them, so the only costs associated with this technique will be the referral fee that you agree to pay.

Technique #23: REI Clubs

Skills: personal presentation

Systems: tracking leads, tracking meetings

Cost: cost of membership

If you are serious about becoming an active and successful

investor, then you need to be involved with any real estate investing clubs in your area. Real estate investing clubs serve as hubs for real estate investors to socialize with one another and educate themselves. As such they are full of all kinds of opportunities.

Your willingness to show up to meetings and interact with the people you meet there even if you are new to the area or to the business almost serves as a litmus test of your ability to succeed as an investor. You won't come across very many opportunities as a recluse, so if the idea of going to these meetings on a regular basis seems daunting to you then that just means that you need to take this opportunity to challenge yourself and overcome whatever is holding you back.

Serious investors get themselves known to other investors and real estate professionals within the community, which is a big part of what allows them to be successful. The more people who know you personally and the more frequently you make contact with others, the more good things have a possibility of coming your way. So if you're not involved with your local REI club already, you should seriously consider it as a way to gain access to great educational opportunities as well as to expose yourself to the body of real estate professionals in your community.

REI club meetings offer a great opportunity to hone your personal presentation skills by meeting lots of real estate professionals in person, so this is a networking technique that will improve these skills as much as it will benefit by them. You don't want the experience to go to waste, however, so you will definitely want to be systematic about organizing and acting on any and all information and contacts you gain at these meetings as well as about attending the meetings themselves; showing up at one meeting or event isn't likely to have much of an effect on your real estate career, but becoming an established presence within these clubs can allow great things to happen.

These clubs typically charge a membership fee on a monthly or yearly basis and may charge for attendance at certain events as well, but the value to cost ratio is likely to be fairly high.

Technique #24: Community Events

Skills: personal presentation

Systems: tracking events, organizing presentations

Cost: highly variable

Something that you should always be looking for as a real estate investor is opportunities to get yourself and your business within view of the public. This is because a lot more deals are going to find their way to you the more people know who you are; this goes for those within the circle of real estate professionals as well as for the community at large.

If your community has any public events that can provide such an opportunity to get noticed you should be aware of them and be ready to act. Any event that will allow you to mingle with the public and market your business is something that you should investigate; examples include street fairs, festivals, sporting events, parades, or any event where you can set up a booth for your business.

Your personal presentation skills, which are important for networking techniques in general, are crucial when it comes to appearing in public and interacting with community members. The better you become at making a favorable impression and delivering your marketing message in person the better the results you will get from applying this technique.

Being organized and systematic about following up with

relevant leads that find their way to you is crucial if you don't want the experience to go to waste, as is keeping up with events in your community and organizing your presentation, whether it includes some sort of a display or is limited to just you giving your sales pitch to as many people as possible. These events may be free or they may have a charge for participation or setting up a booth. You will have to check what is available in your locality to get precise figures.

Find Motivated Sellers: List Based Techniques

As a real estate investor you are not in the business of dealing with tangible products or services in the usual sense. There is no manufacturing involved, and you will not be called upon to perform a personal service for anyone.

Ownership in real estate is purely a matter of convention, since no one can actually pick up a house or a piece of land and carry it off in their possession. On the contrary, the true commodity that is central to your real estate business is information.

Information is the lifeblood that real estate investing thrives on; it is what you are seeking from your prospects and what you are offering to your clients. Therefore it will be helpful to your efforts to further your career to see yourself as also being in the information business.

Also helpful to realize is that a full-time real estate business can not thrive on a meager supply of leads. Leads are the fuel that drives the engine of your business, and without a healthy, steady supply of them your business will stall or starve.

A high volume of leads is crucial no matter what type of deals you do or how many. Whether your business is geared to do a lot of deals with smaller profits on each or fewer deals with higher margins, more leads are always better than fewer because they allow you to be even more selective and strengthen your negotiating position, both of which increase your profit margins.

Think about it, would you rather have one new deal to work in a typical week, or have a choice among 5? And would you do a better job of negotiating a deal if it was the only one you had or if you had a list of alternatives waiting for your attention? The following series of techniques are based on using information sources to your advantage. Although these require an active input of effort to work, they can be used by anyone at any time to generate massive numbers of motivated seller leads.

Technique #25: For Sale Ads

Skills: phone skills

Systems: collecting and tracking leads, placing calls, phone script

Cost: little or none

This is perhaps one of the most basic sources of leads there is. Just open up a newspaper or point your web browser to some online classifieds and look in the real estate or homes for sale section. These types of leads are plentiful and readily available to anybody.

Most of these leads will be no good for investing purposes because the seller isn't motivated and is trying to sell their home for full price to a retail buyer. So look for ads that give clues that the seller is motivated. You might see words like "bring all offers", "must sell", "seller motivated", "investors welcome", "price reduced" or "quick sale wanted".

These types of leads tend to be easy to find and easy to call, so they are a good place to start if you are still building confidence. They will also give you excellent practice in determining a seller's motivation. Remember that there is specific information you want to get from each seller, but you don't want to sound robotic. Therefore you should make a point of speaking naturally and spontaneously on the phone, especially if you are speaking from a script. Becoming too chatty can be a time waster, though, so you will want to keep your conversations directed and somewhat concise.

Perhaps the best thing about these types of leads is that you can find a lot of them in a fairly short period of time at little or no expense. For this reason these can be a good place to start if you are just beginning in real estate. If you're not comfortable talking on the phone yet, this is a good technique to practice that skill. As your ability to talk to sellers on the phone improves, you will see better and better results from using this method.

You should be systematic about collecting these leads, making the calls, and tracking and following up with them. You should also systematize the process of talking to sellers by creating a phone script to follow, or at least a list of talking points and questions to ask every seller you talk to. At first the script will assist your memory to make sure you cover every point, but eventually you won't need it because you will have internalized the system.

There are no costs associated with this method, other than perhaps the cost of a newspaper.

Technique #26: For Rent Ads

Skills: phone skills

Systems: collecting and tracking leads, placing calls, phone script

Cost: little or none

Your local print or online classifieds also contain another valuable lead source that many investors overlook. While you are prospecting from the "homes for sale" section, you can also mine the "homes for rent" section for tons of good leads.

Unlike the "homes for sale" section, where you want to screen for seller motivation, almost all of these are worth calling. The reason, as discussed in technique #2, is that all landlords are potential motivated sellers. Even if they're not interested in selling the property they're advertising, they may have others that they are trying to get rid of, or they might be interested in buying some new ones, which you can hopefully help them out with as well. So just open up any classified to the "homes for rent" section and call through the ads systematically and you are bound to come across a few deals.

Don't hesitate to be forthcoming about your status as an investor. Remember, these people are professional investors too, or at least semi-professional, and they are likely to recognize and be turned off by any attempt to pull the wool over their eyes about your true motivations. Some investors like these types of leads best of all because landlords are not likely to be as emotional about their properties as homeowners can be, so the conversations tend to be strictly business and straight to the point.

As your phone skills improve so will your success with this method. Your negotiation skills will also come in handy to convince the landlord to sell instead of renting. The processes of collecting these leads, placing the calls, tracking and following up should all be systematized to ensure consistency. The process of talking to landlords should also be systematized with a phone script or list of talking points until you have it down by heart.

Technique #27: MLS

Skills: computer skills, phone skills

Systems: collecting and tracking leads, placing calls, phone script

Cost: little or none

The multiple listing service, or MLS, used by licensed real estate agents shouldn't be overlooked as a source of leads, considering that the vast majority (over 90%) of properties sold are listed on the MLS. The only catch will be gaining access. In some localities this simply won't be possible without being a licensed real estate agent, while in others the contents of the MLS are made publicly available. If you are friendly you might even be able to buddy up with a real estate agent to share access.

If you can gain access to the MLS it can be a valuable source of market data as well as leads; just keep in mind that in most markets the sale prices of properties average 6% to 10% below the original listing prices, so MLS listings in a neighborhood will tend to run a little higher than actual sales in the same neighborhood.

There are several ways to find deals on the MLS: you can look for listings that indicate investment properties or motivated sellers, you can look for listings that are very old or that have already expired or are about to expire, or you can make very low offers on a large number of properties and hope to get lucky.

If you have the time and the tools you can comb the MLS frequently throughout the day for new listings. Often true bargains appear on the MLS and disappear within a matter of hours or even minutes because they are quickly snapped up by eager buyers. If you can get the jump on one of these it can turn into an easy deal.

The MLS database is huge, and the more computer-savvy you are the easier time you will have making sense of it. Thus improving your computer skills as well as your phone skills can improve your performance with this technique. The systems you should have in place are ones for collecting and tracking leads, placing calls, and talking with selling agents (since each property is listed with an agent, you won't be talking to the sellers directly). There should be no cost for using the MLS, assuming you are able to gain access to it.

Technique #28: Notice of Default List

Skills: phone skills

Systems: collecting and tracking leads, skip tracing, placing calls, phone script

Cost: variable but fairly cheap

This is a lead source that is of particular use to pre-foreclosure investors. When a mortgage on a property becomes delinquent, a notice of default is filed with the county by the lender. These notices of default are published in a notice of default list, or lis pendens list, every month by the county which gives the addresses of properties with defaulted mortgages and the names of the owners. Many of these owners are motivated sellers or soon will be, and a little skip tracing will allow you to contact them directly.

These lists are actually fairly commonly distributed and easy to come by, but not all of them you find will be completely up-to-date, and some of them may have already been picked through and contain only the leads that another investor didn't want! There are multiple sources of these lists online, which tend to be the least reliable. You should be able to get one that's more accurate by simply asking a title company.

The most up-to-date and accurate list will be the one you get by visiting the county courthouse in person, although this also takes the most time. If you intend to work with sellers in pre-foreclosure as part of your business strategy, this is the primary source for them, and there are plenty.

Acquiring leads this way is dependent on your ability to talk to homeowners in pre-foreclosure on the phone, so as you improve this skill you will have better and better success with this technique. You should have systems in place for collecting and tracking the leads and skip tracing the homeowners to find phone numbers, as well as a systematic method of placing the calls and a pre-defined script to follow during the conversation. If you get the list from the county courthouse it should be free, but other sources may charge for it.

Technique #29: Probate Court

Skills: research, phone skills, empathy

Systems: collecting and tracking leads, mailing letters, placing calls, phone script

Cost: little or none

As mentioned in technique # 8, properties that have been inherited or that belonged to someone who is recently deceased can be excellent deals, because they are often a burden to the person who inherits them or who is in charge of settling the affairs of the estate (this person is called the executor). The process of transferring the assets of a deceased person is called probate, and it is handled through the probate court system.

Probate leads take patience to work. For one thing, published lists of probate properties are rare; usually the closest you can come is to acquire a list of wills in probate (made publicly available by the county records office or courthouse) and contact the executors of wills that contain real estate. The contact can be made by phone or by mail. For another thing, sibling rivalry is common when one heir wants to sell the property and another one doesn't, or when the heirs are not able to agree on a sale price.

On top of that, you can not ordinarily purchase a property out of probate, but must wait until after the probate process is complete. However, while a property is in probate you can still get in touch with the executor and make an offer to buy the property once the process is completed. If you are able to build rapport with the executor and come to an agreement then it is just a matter of waiting. These types of leads rarely proceed quickly, but the payoff can be worth the wait, especially if you have a steady supply of them in your pipeline.

A few specific skills are involved with obtaining these types of leads. One of these is the ability to do research, as the executors of wills in probate usually take some legwork to find. Another is the ability to talk with the executor on the phone and convince them to work with you. And since the executors of wills are often concurrently going through a process of grieving, this is a situation where a little bit of empathy can go a long way.

By improving these skills you will be able to improve your rate of success with this technique. Systems are especially important for collecting these leads as well as tracking them, and also for mailing letters and/or placing phone calls. A phone script is also useful for being systematic about how you talk with the sellers and gather information. Other than the time cost involved, the process of obtaining these leads is essentially free.

Technique #30: Housing Court

Skills: phone skills

Systems: collecting and tracking leads, placing calls, phone script

Cost: little or none

Housing court is the place where landlords have to file for evictions of tenants who don't pay the rent. If you can get a list from the county courthouse of landlords who have filed for evictions you will have a great marketing tool. These landlords are more likely to be burned out or disgruntled than ones you find at random through the classifieds or by driving neighborhoods, because they are currently going through the headache of an eviction, and thus they are more likely to be motivated to sell.

Call them and talk to them and you may even find that they have a number of properties that they are ready to get rid of. Landlording can be a tough occupation and many who try give up in disgust sometime after they have to unplug their thousandth toilet or so. And whether they do want to sell or they don't, it is usually possible to talk frankly with them and get right to the point so that you can move on to the next call.

Your skill at building rapport over the phone is what will make this technique work for you, so improving your phone skills will improve your success rate. A systematic approach is essential to collecting and tracking these leads and also to placing the calls so that you don't get burned out. A phone script or list of talking points will systematically ensure that you say the right things and gather the right information when talking to these potential sellers.

Technique #31: Bankruptcy Court

Skills: phone skills

Systems: collecting and tracking leads, placing calls, mailing letters, phone script

Cost: little or none

Thousands of homeowners go into bankruptcy every month, and many of these will become motivated sellers either before or after the bankruptcy is over. When an owner files bankruptcy a hold is placed on all collection activity against them, so if their property is in foreclosure this may be stopped temporarily. However, the bankruptcy court will work out a new payment arrangement with their creditors, and if they default on this new arrangement then they will lose bankruptcy protection for their house. This is the point at which they are most likely to become motivated sellers.

If you are in the pre-foreclosure business you can help these people the same way you would help a seller in pre-foreclosure. The only difference is how you get the lead. Your local county courthouse will provide you with a list of records of people who have filed bankruptcy, which you can cross-reference with your local county appraisal district to find out which ones of them are property owners.

Usually a combination of calling these sellers and sending them letters in the mail will be most effective. They are probably used to hiding from creditors, so they may be a little bit reclusive until they become ready to work with somebody, which is often right at the last minute. Patience and multiple follow ups are essential to turning these leads into deals.

How well you are able to build rapport with sellers over the phone will partly determine how well this technique will work for you, so you will get better at this as your phone skills improve. The systems you should have in place for this type of marketing are systems for collecting and tracking the leads, placing calls, and mailing letters to homeowners in bankruptcy. As is usually the case when you are cold-calling you should talk on the phone with a phone script or talking point list in front of you, at least until you have the routine down.

Technique #32: Code Violation Office

Skills: phone skills

Systems: collecting and tracking leads, skip tracing, placing calls, phone script

Cost: little or none

Depending on where you live, either municipal or county authorities regularly inspect all buildings for building code violations. You can often spot these properties while you are driving around in your target market because they will have a violation notice posted visibly on them. You can also obtain a list of these properties by petitioning the appropriate city or county code office. (Since these properties are likely to be abandoned, this can be a great way to acquire a list of abandoned properties as well.)

You may have to do some skip tracing in order to contact the owners, but once you do there is a good chance that the lead will turn into a deal. Think about it: if the owner doesn't have the interest to maintain the property up to code, it's unlikely they are interested in either keeping it indefinitely or selling it for top dollar.

Phone skills are important in getting the owners of these properties to talk to you and agree to sell their property, so as your phone skills improve, so will your success rate with applying this technique. You will want to have a system in place for collecting and tracking these leads, just like any other, as well as for skip tracing if it is necessary to locate the owners. You will also want to have a systematic process for placing the calls so that you don't just do a whole bunch one time and then never do any more (has this ever happened to you with anything)?

In addition to these systems you will also want to have a phone script or list of talking points ready to ensure that you are systematic about how you talk to these owners and that you make the same relevant points and gather the same relevant information with each phone call. Since the list of code violations is a matter of public record, this technique is essentially free to apply.

Technique #33: Bank REO Departments

Skills: phone skills, negotiation

Systems: collecting and tracking leads, placing calls, phone script

Cost: little or none

We all know that when a mortgage lender forecloses on a property, the deed to the property is placed on the auction block at the monthly foreclosure sale. What you might not know, however, is that at these auctions most of the properties are not sold. These properties then belong to the lender and are classified as REOs, or Real Estate Owned.

This is a much better time to make an offer to buy a property than at the foreclosure auction, unless you happen to like bidding against lots of other investors on properties that are already overpriced to begin with. Once the property becomes an REO, you will have much more negotiating power with the lender. The basic reason is that lenders do not want to own properties.

For one thing, the longer a lender owns a property the more it costs them, because they become responsible for the taxes, insurance, and management of the property, not to mention having to pay a real estate commission when it finally does sell. For another thing, most mortgage lenders don't actually have the money they lend; they get their money from the Federal Reserve, which prints it. But a bank is penalized for every REO it has on its books, which means that it has less money available to lend. So banks are strongly motivated to get rid of their REOs and become more so the longer they hold them.

This is, of course, great news for you as an investor, because it means that all you have to do is contact any bank or mortgage lender and request a list of their REO properties, then make lowball offers on as many of them as you please. The catch is that lenders will usually only sell these properties to a cash buyer and will want to see a POF (proof of funds) before they will even look at your offer. In addition, lenders will not accept a closing by assignment, so if you do business as a wholesaler you can't generally assign a contract for such a property. If you can overcome these hurdles, however, making offers on REOs is akin to being a kid in a candy store.

When making offers on REO properties your skills at building rapport over the phone will get your foot in the door, but banks tend to be tough negotiators so your negotiation skills will be crucial to turning these leads into deals. The systems involved in this process are ones for collecting and tracking the leads, placing the calls to lenders, and a phone script or list of talking points to keep you on track in your discussion with the lender. Although you must show that you have cash in order to buy these properties, acquiring the leads is absolutely free.

Technique #34: Fire-Damaged Homes

Skills: phone skills, negotiation

Systems: collecting and tracking leads, skip tracing, placing calls, phone script

Cost: little or none

Many times when a home is severely damaged by fire, the homeowners would rather just sell it and find a new one than go to the trouble of repairing the old one. You can find sellers in this situation by obtaining a list of fire-damaged homes.

And where would you find such a list? If you answered "from the fire department", score yourself 10 points and move ahead one space. The list you get is likely to contain only addresses, so you should be prepared to do some skip tracing to actually get in contact with the owners of these properties. And if you convince them to sell to you, be sure to get a copy of their homeowner's insurance policy. After the transaction is completed, as the rightful new owner of the property you might be able to file a claim with the insurance company, and receive money for the damages, which will go directly into your bottom line.

Your phone skills will be what scores you these leads; as you improve at talking with potential sellers over the phone you will be able to make this technique work more and more in your favor. A systematic process should be implemented for collecting and tracking these leads, as usual, and also for skip tracing and making the calls. And just like any other time you have to have the same phone conversation over and over again, you should come up with a phone script or list of talking points to keep your conversations focused and on track. The cost of obtaining these leads: $0.

Technique #35: Absentee Owners

Skills: phone skills, negotiation

Systems: collecting and tracking leads, placing calls, phone script

Cost: cheap, dependent upon volume

Absentee owners are simply defined as owners who do not live in the property under consideration. This is a fairly broad classification and can include landlords, people who own second homes, and people who simply have an extra house that's sitting unused because they don't know what to do with it.

An absentee owner could live in a different state or just across the street. Basically the only thing that absentee owners have in common is a house that they aren't using themselves at least part of the time. Any of these owners could be motivated to sell for one reason or another, but you won't know whether or not they are until you call them and find out.

Unlike some of the other types of lists we've been considering, absentee owner lists are not compiled as a matter of public record. You could theoretically compile one yourself from combing through county tax appraisal district records, but this would be quite time consuming, especially if you are working in a county where the records have not yet been moved online.

The easiest way to obtain such a list is from a list broker. List brokers have access to all kinds of public information and the software to process it, and they can compile complete marketing lists according to just about any criteria you care to stipulate. A list broker will charge for this information, of course, but there are plenty of them out there and you can shop around to get the best price.

Implementing this technique relies on your skill at talking with sellers on the phone, but you may also have to use some of your negotiation skills up front to get the lead because the absentee owner might not be willing to sell initially. As you get better at talking with sellers over the phone and negotiating you will get better at using this technique as well.

You should have systems ready to collect and track these leads and place the calls, as well as a phone script to keep you on track with your agenda when talking with absentee owners. If things get too chatty and you forget what you're supposed to say or ask, you'll not only waste time, you may waste the lead as well. The cost of having such a list compiled will depend on the size of the list you order, but it shouldn't be prohibitively expensive, in the neighborhood of a few cents per lead.

Technique #36: Aged FSBOs

Skills: phone skills

Systems: collecting and tracking leads, placing calls, phone script

Cost: little or none

This technique is almost the same as technique #25, but with a twist: instead of looking in this week's paper for houses for sale, look in a paper from three to twelve months ago. "But won't most of the houses be sold already?" you might ask? Indeed they will, and that's the point. Most of the houses will be sold, but some won't be. And if the seller still has the house after three to twelve months of trying to sell it, then the seller might just be motivated enough to cut you a deal.

The same principle operates in this lead source as in many others: if there's a chance that an owner in that situation might be motivated to sell, then probability dictates that if you talk to enough owners in that situation, some of them will be motivated to sell. It's simple math. It's also simple to get your hands on some aged classifieds; if you don't have any newspapers that old, start saving them (at least the classifieds). And in the meantime ask a friend or go to the library and browse their newspaper collection.

Your skills at using the phone to talk to sellers will contribute to how well this technique works for you, so keep honing them. Your results will also depend on the systems you have in place for collecting and tracking these leads (like saving your classifieds, for example), and placing new calls regularly. A phone script or list of talking points to assist your memory will also contribute to your success with this technique, and can be refined as you gain experience.

Technique #37: Section 8 Landlord List

Skills: phone skills

Systems: collecting and tracking leads, placing calls, phone script

Cost: little or none

The Section 8 Housing Authority is a government bureau that helps low-income tenants pay their rents. This turns out to be an alright deal for the landlord as well, because the Section 8 Housing Authority ensures the timeliness of the landlord's rental payments and insures the landlord's property against damages. This is why so many landlords sign up with Section 8.

In fact, so many landlords sign up with Section 8 that the Section 8 Housing Authority has a big, long list of them, and they will give you a copy if you ask them nicely. Just look up the Section 8 Housing Authority in your area. These are just landlord leads and you should handle them the same way you would handle any others (see techniques # 2, # 26, & # 30).

The better your skills of presentation over the phone the better you'll be able to find deals this way. Other than calling them up and talking there's not much to getting these leads. But you should have systems in place to collect and track these or any leads that come into your office if you plan to handle a lot of them. Systems for calling are also important if you plan to be making a large number of calls, including a phone script or a list of talking points with the exact information you want to give to and receive from the seller. Your good fortune is such that this technique for generating leads is exactly free.

Finding Motivated Sellers: Places To Advertise

Farming the neighborhood, networking, and prospecting lists are all valuable strategies for bringing leads into your real estate business, and your overall marketing plan should include elements from all of them, but if your marketing plan consisted only of these activities, it would still be incomplete.

Farming and working with lists can generate large numbers of leads, but they take time to carry out and require active participation. If for some reason you became occupied working on a super hot deal and stopped farming or prospecting for a week your source of new leads would dry up and your business would come to a halt. Networking will generate leads passively for you after you have laid the groundwork, but it takes time for this source of leads to build up to an appreciable volume. The strategy that can fill this gap is good, old-fashioned advertising: you place an ad, a prospect sees it, and they call.

The advantage of advertising is that you can generate a large number of leads quickly and passively, so new deals can be coming into your office while you are working on other things. The drawback is that you must pay for the leads, and some of these methods can become quite expensive. Nevertheless, finding advertising solutions that will fit your budget and still be effective is well worth the effort because it can free up your time for other equally important things (like closing deals, for example).

The following series of techniques all have to do with advertising your business. Some of them are more commonly used than others, but all of them can bring you leads. Traditionally real estate investors tend to advertise in a few common places, but advertising opportunities abound and are limited only by your imagination. If you can come up with something that hasn't been tried before in your area then the very novelty of it can work in your favor. So don't limit yourself to the possibilities described here. You should always be looking for new venues for your marketing message.

Technique #38: Newspaper Classifieds

Skills: designing marketing messages

Systems: placing ads, answering calls, tracking leads

Cost: variable, around $10-$100 per week

This is a classic staple of the real estate investor's advertising diet. Done to death but reliable, this old standby can be counted on to net you at least a half dozen deals a year if run consistently, which will more than pay for itself in the long run.

With newspaper advertising rates being as expensive as they

are, it might not be the best technique to use on a limited budget, and it certainly isn't the best technique to use all by itself. When you have extra money in your advertising budget, though, you should give it a try. One detail to keep in mind is that whatever phone number you run in this ad should be answered by a person, not a machine, because your ad will be surrounded by other similar ads, so if a person calling it doesn't get an answer they will most likely not even bother to leave a message and just sell their house to someone who picks up the phone when they call.

Because your ad will be surrounded by other similar ads, this is one instance where a unique and well- crafted marketing message can really make a difference. You should try experimenting with different variations over time to see what pulls best; in this way you can improve your skill at designing marketing messages while simultaneously improving your results. Naturally you will want to have a systematic approach for placing these ads, as well as answering the calls that they draw and tracking and following up with the leads that they bring into your office.

Technique #39: Online Classifieds

Skills: designing marketing messages

Systems: placing ads, answering calls, tracking leads

Cost: very cheap or free

Online classifieds are a lot like print classifieds, except for the facts that they allow you to use as much text as you want to write your ad, they can potentially be seen by a wider range of prospects, and they are free.

Actually, come to think of it, online classifieds are quite a bit different from paper classifieds. They have all of the advantages mentioned, plus chances are good that you can find more than one of them in your local area. The two most popular ones are www.craigslist.org and www.backpage.com, but others abound. If you are starting out on a limited budget then online classifieds are probably much more practical for you than print classifieds would be. Otherwise, they serve the same purpose, and if you ignore all of the differences, they're the same.

As within other advertising media, a well-designed ad will pull well here while a poorly-designed ad will pull less well. Fortunately for you designing marketing messages is a skill that you can work to improve over time. The systems that you use for placing these ads, answering the calls generated, and tracking the leads that come from them will be similar to the systems that you use for print classifieds and other advertising techniques, except without the spending money part.

Technique #40: Radio Ads

Skills: designing marketing messages

Systems: placing ads, answering calls, tracking leads

Cost: low to high hundreds of $

This is a marketing medium that a few real estate investors are starting to move into, at least in some cities, but you still may be able to be the first real estate investor to advertise on the radio in your area. You should shop around, but you shouldn't choose a slot to run your ad based on price alone. The ratings, i.e. the number of people listening, and the demographic makeup of the audience should factor into the decision as well. If you pay for the cheapest time slot you can find then you'll get what you pay for.

Another factor to consider is the programming that is going on during your ad. Running your radio ad during a news show is probably better than running it during a music program, because people are probably more likely to be listening to it, rather than just having it on as background noise. The best way to learn which time slots work best for you is to do your own experiments by running ads at different times and tracking the results.

Designing a marketing message for a radio ad is a unique skill, one that you can improve with practice, experience, and, of course, experimentation. As you get better at this your results with this technique will improve. Your systems should allow you to keep up with placing the advertisements, answer the calls you get, and track and follow up with the leads automatically, without having to think about it. This is one of the more expensive advertising options available, but not out of reach of a medium-sized advertising budget.

Technique #41: Television Ads

Skills: designing marketing messages

Systems: placing ads, answering calls, tracking leads

Cost: low hundreds to thousands of $

"Wait", you may be asking, "Isn't television advertising expensive?" Yes, relative to the other techniques listed here, but not as expensive as you might think. It will vary widely depending on the location, station, and time slot, and can actually be quite affordable for a medium sized advertising budget. With hundreds of channels on cable and satellite and more being created all the time, there's lots of advertising space for sale.

And despite the cost, there are two major advantages of

television advertising. One is that it will get your ad viewed by a large number of potential prospects if you choose the timeslot well. The other is that a television advertisement conveys the image of a prestigious, reliable company, which will help to build your reputation. So television advertising is worth experimenting with when you have the extra dollars in your budget from all the free lead generation techniques you now know, and in the mean time it is worth calling some local television stations to check on their rates.

Designing a marketing message for television will invoke at least a few skills you will be able to find ways to improve at. Systems for placing and monitoring your advertising will be essential, as well as for answering the large volume of calls you will receive if you apply this technique effectively, and also tracking the resulting leads. In general you can expect the cost of using this advertising method to be from a few hundred dollars up into the thousands.

Technique #42: Outdoor Advertising

Skills: designing marketing messages

Systems: placing marketing ads, answering calls, tracking leads

Cost: varies widely, low hundreds to thousands of $

Bandit signs are the most basic way to advertise outside, but there are lots of others that range from the mundane to the fanciful (not to mention legitimate). Chances are that the more you look for outdoor advertising space when you are around your target market the more opportunities you will see to implement it.

If your city has a bus system, for example, chances are that you can place ads on the bus benches, as well as on the buses themselves. If real estate agents and lawyers can do it, why not investors? Billboards are another example, but these are among the most costly forms of outdoor advertising; you shouldn't consider including them in your marketing budget unless you're prepared to handle the big guns and do a large volume of business.

As with other forms of advertising, your skill at designing a compelling marketing message will determine to a large extent how well your outdoor advertising will work, so this is an area in which seeking personal improvement will pay off. The systems that you use for placing this type of advertising are likely to be hired ones, but you should definitely have a phone system in place that is capable of capturing and processing a volume of calls proportional to the scale of your advertising efforts. (That means that you shouldn't purchase a billboard and expect to take all of the calls on your cell phone.) the cost of implementing outdoor advertising will vary widely depending on the location, type, and other factors, from the low hundreds of dollars into the thousands.

Technique #43: Telephone Book Ads

Skills: designing marketing messages

Systems: placing ads, answering calls, tracking leads

Cost: variable, check local rates

Here's a place you have probably always seen advertising but never thought about it: on the inside and outside covers of the telephone book. Ever wonder how many calls those attorneys get all year from having their ad on every phone book in the city?

Chances are the other investors in your area haven't thought of this yet, so you get to be the first. If so it's not because it won't get calls, it's only because they are uncreative. Or it could be that they are simply content with the advertising that everybody else uses, but this doesn't describe you, does it? If you can advertise in a manner or in a location that no other businesses like yours are using then you can take advantage of a unique level of visibility (assuming, of course, that the location is one that actually gets looked at by prospects from your target market).

The uniqueness of the placement of your ad will give it an advantage (at least until others start to take after your example), but your success with this technique will still depend on your skill at designing a compelling marketing message, which is something that you have the capability to improve over time. It will also depend on how efficient you are at designing systems to place the ads, answer the calls that they draw, and track the leads that result from them, which can be improved with time. The cost of these ads will vary depending on locality, so you should check locally for advertising rates.

Technique #44: Direct Mail

Skills: designing marketing messages

Systems: sending mailings, answering calls, tracking leads

Cost: variable, dependent on volume

Direct mail is another mainstay of advertising for real estate investors. This type of advertising is not displayed before the general public, but instead is mailed to specific prospects, and is thus best used in conjunction with a targeted list of some kind.

Direct mail has a number of benefits that have kept it in use for a long time. One of these is that it can be targeted for a specific type of homeowner and can even be personalized with an individual's name. Another is that it allows for quite a bit of creativity in the design of the marketing material. A third is that it is highly scalable, meaning that you can spend a little and do a little or spend a lot and do a lot, with results that scale in proportion to the investment. This makes it ideal for a steadily growing business. And, finally, it bypasses cold calling altogether; the sellers call you when they are ready to talk, instead of the other way around.

However, this is a slower lead generation process than prospecting, because many of the leads generated by the mailings take some time to come back, and because most of them never come back at all. It is necessary to send a large number of mail pieces in order to get consistent leads; as a rule of thumb, plan for the response rate to be between 1% and 5% and you should be okay.

The implementation of this technique is a great way to let your creativity flow into your marketing message and is a great way to increase your skill. The more compelling your marketing message is the better the response rate will be to your mailings. The systems necessary to implement this technique are ones to send out the mailings, answer the calls that come in, and track the leads you receive. The cost of implementing this technique will be the cost for the marketing piece (plus postage) times the number of pieces you send. You can spend a little and send a little or spend a lot and send a lot, but figure for no more than $1-$5 for each piece of mail.

Technique #45: Magazines

Skills: designing marketing messages

Systems: placing ads, answering calls, tracking leads

Cost: variable, check local rates

Another print medium that can get your marketing message in front of a targeted audience is magazines. Magazine advertising has the advantage that the audience demographic is fairly well defined, so your ad can be specialized for the audience that will be seeing it. And there are so many different magazines on so many specialized subjects that there is a wide selection to choose from: just about every kind of business, hobby, or interest you can imagine is probably the subject of a magazine. In addition to specialty magazines, national magazines like Time and Newsweek usually have regional editions, so you can have your ad appear in a nationwide magazine but only be viewable in your local area.

Whatever type of market you want to target, remember that magazines are everywhere, and a dedicated search will probably find several that will reach exactly the type of homeowner you are looking for. It is important to define your intended prospects as specifically as possible, not only to select the appropriate publications but also to design your marketing message with these prospects in mind.

Your skill at designing marketing messages will make this technique work for you, and the success you have with this technique will improve as this skill improves. The systems necessary to implement this technique effectively are ones you design for placing ads, answering the phone when the calls come in, and tracking the leads that you get from advertising this way. The cost will vary widely depending on the publication but no matter what your budget you should be able to find at least a few cost effective options.

Technique #46: Neighborhood Publications

Skills: finding publications, designing, marketing messages

Systems: placing ads, answering calls, tracking leads

Cost: variable but cheap, check local rates

As you become more and more familiar with your target market you will become aware of various neighborhood organizations that publish newsletters and other publications. These types of organizations usually sell advertising space to local businesses, which can add to your arsenal of techniques for reaching your target market with your marketing message.

Examples of these types of organizations abound: clubs like Kiwanis and Rotary, Bar associations, schools, churches, sports clubs, hobby groups, and business associations, to point out just a few. Look for these types of organizations in your area, and contact them to ask about advertising in their newsletter. If you happen to be a member of any of these organizations yourself, you should probably start with that one. You might not get a large volume of leads with this method, but the ones you do get should be qualified and cost-effective. As an added benefit, having your ad seen in many of these publications will add to your positive image in the neighborhood.

Finding neighborhood publications is a skill you can improve at with practice, as is designing a marketing message that is compelling to your target market. As you get better at these skills you will have better success with this method. You should have systems in place by the time you get started for placing the ads, answering the calls you receive from them, and tracking the leads that you obtain this way. The rates for this type of advertising will vary widely, but you can expect it to be easily affordable.

Finding Motivated Sellers: The Internet

In the real estate business, many of the fundamentals have remained unchanged for decades: things like identifying motivated sellers, negotiating, and designing compelling marketing messages, for example. However, the influence of the Internet has been pervasive in all facets of modern life and commerce, and this has affected the world of real estate as well. The Internet is as essential to life and business today as the telephone.

As you will no doubt recall from earlier, real estate is an information based business, and the Internet has made an enormous amount of information widely available. Slowly but surely this explosion of information and electronic commerce is changing the face of the real estate industry. In particular, as an investor you can use the Internet as a medium for networking, finding deals, finding buyers, and distributing information about yourself and your business.

True, using the Internet doesn't replace the need to master fundamentals, and there is a lot more to running a business than just putting up a website. Still, the wealth of information and technology that the Internet makes available is subtly shaping the nature of the investing game as we speak, and will continue to do so for a long time to come. If you don't at least have a finger in the Internet pie you will eventually find your business model becoming obsolete. The following series of techniques all involve harnessing the power of the Internet to bring deals to your business.

Technique #47: Lead Generating Services

Skills: phone skills

Systems: collecting and tracking leads

Cost: fairly cheap, but varies

In the modern economy almost anything can be turned into a service, and finding leads for real estate investors is no different. There are a large number of services that will provide leads to real estate investors on some sort of paid basis. These include sites like www.rehablist.com that are nationwide as well as ones that are specific to a local market.

Some will provide pre-foreclosure leads, some will supply leads for motivated sellers that have responded to some sort of advertising, and some will supply wholesale deals or almost any other type of lead you can imagine. Some charge a monthly membership fee for unlimited access, while some will charge a certain fee per lead. Some distribute a general list of all leads to all members, while some will distribute individual leads to single members only.

Like other techniques listed here, this one should be used in conjunction with several other lead sources, as you are not likely to get all of the business you need just from subscribing to one of these services. Also, it is important to be discriminating and make sure that you are getting sufficient value from what you are paying for; all lead generating services are not created equal, and some are golden while some are a waste of money.

While finding and signing up for one of these services is a fairly simple proposition that requires little if any specialized skills, how successful you are at following up with the leads will be dependent upon your skill at talking to sellers on the phone, so there is plenty of opportunity for improvement. Also, while the service will supply you with the leads, following up with and tracking them will be your responsibility, and you should have systems in place for doing this faultlessly. The cost of such a service varies quite a bit, but none of them are prohibitively expensive, usually being under $100 per month.

Technique #48: Social Networking Sites

Skills: designing marketing messages, networking

Systems: tracking leads

Cost: little or none

While social networking sites were originally developed for leisure purposes, the ability of these types of sites to build massive online communities and get in touch with large numbers of people on a regular basis didn't go unnoticed by entrepreneurs for long.

The best-known social networking sites today are probably Twitter and Facebook, and plenty of businesses have established their presence within these networks. However, there are also a plethora of specialized social networking sites designed for business professionals in general or for one certain type of business in particular. One such example for the real estate community is www.realestateinvestor.com. Establishing a profile on one or more of these sites and making a continual effort to grow your list of contacts is one quick and easy way to establish an online presence and build your network of real estate professionals.

While social networking sites require no specialized skills to set up and operate, crafting your marketing message and growing your network is up to you, and fortunately these are skills that allow room for growth and improvement. And while a social networking site is its own system, any leads that come through applying this technique should go into your system to be tracked and followed up like any other. The costs associated with applying this technique are minimal. Many social networking sites are free, while those that are specialized for a particular industry may charge a nominal membership fee.

Technique #49: Website

Skills: designing, marketing, messages, web design

Systems: tracking leads

Cost: hosting fee, design fee

While your real estate business may or may not have a physical office that is open to the public, it can have a virtual office where any interested parties may point their browsers to learn about and get in contact with your company. The basic functions of a website are twofold: to provide information about you and your business to visitors, and to allow prospects or potential clients to get in touch with you regarding your services.

As such, your website should contain as much information that might be relevant to your visitors as possible and should provide them with the means to contact you at least by phone and email. A good website can actually do much more than this, but this is the minimum functionality it should have.

Just putting up a website does not guarantee that you will receive traffic; it is necessary to ensure that web traffic has a way to reach your site. Various forms of advertising can accomplish this, as can getting your site ranked highly with the major search engines.

Designing a website and optimizing it to receive search engine traffic are tasks best handled by an expert, so you can either become an expert or you can hire one. Also among your options are designing a website from scratch or selecting and customizing a pre-designed website specialized for real estate investors. My company Real Estate Websites To Go http://www.realestatewebsitestogo.info offers custom made real estate investor websites templates that are designed to attract motivated sellers, motivated buyers, wholesale investors and private lenders.

We currently have a super special going on where you get 4 websites for $1 initially as well as a 30 day free trial to try us out. If you like our websites and we are sure that you will, you pay only $39.99 per month for 4 websites that will help you find, attract and pre-screen all of your leads.

Technique #50: Tax Deeds

Skills: bidding at auction

Systems: researching properties

Cost: little or none

This final technique stands in a category by itself. More than just a way of finding leads, tax deeds are actually a method of buying properties and an entire investing subject all to themselves. The basic rundown of how the process works is as follows.

All property owners have to pay property taxes to the county taxing authority each year. If a property owner fails to pay these taxes, the property becomes tax defaulted and subject to seizure by the county authorities. In order to raise money the county will sell these properties at auction, starting the bidding at the amount of the taxes owed. As an investor, this can make it possible for you to acquire the property at a massive discount, because the yearly taxes owed on a property are usually a small fraction of its total value. (For example, in California property taxes are fixed at 1% of the most recent purchase price of the property.)

The great thing is that a tax foreclosure wipes out almost any other liens that are attached to the property. This means that if a property with a $500,000 mortgage attached is foreclosed on for $5,000 of back taxes and sold at a county tax auction, the mortgage will be wiped out, leaving the new owner with a free-and-clear property.

The process does have a few small catches however. One is that the properties are sold at auction to cash buyers only, so in order to purchase them you have to bid against other investors and pay cash up front. Another is the redemption period. When the county taxing authority seizes a property, the original owner has a redemption period (the length of time varies by state) during which they can make up the delinquent taxes plus penalties and reclaim the property. This means that when you purchase a property this way you may not end up with the property itself but rather with your money back plus some interest.

Even with these stipulations, tax deed investing can be a very lucrative activity if you are prepared to do your research and pay cash. Information about tax deed auctions and lists of properties for sale can be acquired from your local county administration center.

Bidding at auctions is a very particular skill, and the better you become at it the more successful you can be with this technique. Taking a systematic approach to identifying and researching properties, particularly with regard to title issues, will also pay off well. And while you do have to pay cash for these properties, acquiring the leads themselves and bidding at the auction is free.

Scripts for Your Motivated Seller Prospects

In some of the aforementioned techniques we've explored I indicated that it is necessary to use scripts to communicate with motivated sellers. As a result of your marketing you will inevitably start receiving calls from potential motivated seller prospects. Shouldn't you know exactly what to say to pre-screen them and eventually close the deal? Of course you should, because the bottom line is your success as a real-estate investor hinges on your ability to effectively communicate with motivated sellers.

When you know exactly what to say to the motivated sellers that you encounter, you will close deals and make a ton of cash. On the other hand, if you nervously fumble and stutter because you're at a loss for words you will never close any deals and make any money. It's that simple.

The drawbacks of talking to sellers without knowing what to say especially when you are still at the beginning of your learning curve are many fold. It is all around bad for your business and bad for your morale. If you don't know the most important things to say when you are on the phone with sellers to get the results that you want, you will waste a lot of time and good deals.

If you presently have any experience as a real estate investor, have you ever tried to talk to sellers and had any of these types of problems?

*The seller makes an objection that you don't have a satisfactory response too.

*The seller asks you a question that you can't answer.

*You don't know what questions you should be asking in order to get the information you need.

*You don't know what type of offer to make after the seller

has explained their situation so you have to get off the phone without making an offer promising to call back later.

*You are having a hard time persuading sellers to accept your offers.

These types of problems alone will make things difficult for you in your real-estate business. But they will also harm your morale making it so that talking to sellers comes to be an activity that you fear and dread, which is a dead end street for sure. Without a doubt, if you are not able to develop the ability to talk to sellers comfortably and naturally with the minimum of anxiety and stress and with maximum skill and effectiveness, success with real-estate is not likely to be in your future.

Would you go to a job interview unprepared? Would you give a public speech off the top of your head? Would you run a marathon without practicing? Just as silly as all of these things would be to talk to sellers without knowing what to say. Having a pre-written script memorized before talking to sellers will not only allow you to sound like you know what you are talking about, even if you don't at first, it will explode the effectiveness of your negotiations by eliminating the aforementioned problems as well as by giving you the confidence that comes with knowing what you are going to say rather than having to invent it as you go along.

This is not to say that you wouldn't eventually become skillful at talking to sellers through trial and error alone assuming you had enough chances to practice, plenty of patience, and all the time in the world to make it work, but having the benefit of a comprehensive collection of pre-written scripts dealing with any seller and any type of situation can drastically shorten your learning curve and therefore increase your effectiveness in a much shorter period of time than if you had to reinvent the wheel. Remember that even the President speaks from scripts, but don't let this stop you from doing it.

The truth is that we all have our own scripts that we use unconsciously in any situation. If you make 30 phone calls to 30 sellers, you would inevitably find yourself repeating the same thing over and over and over again. The question is, are the scripts that you already have to talking to sellers the most effective ones you could be using?

Most likely they are not unless they had been polished through education and experience. And the most benefit comes from actually memorizing the script, knowing it like you know the words of your favorite song or the pledged allegiance. Studies have shown that memorizing the script, perhaps changing the wording here and there so that you feel more comfortable with it, but keeping the main points intact is more effective than simply having an outline or a broad idea of what you want to be saying.

So, even if you have experience talking to sellers, you would still benefit from having the exact words and phrases you need on the tip of your tongue and ready to be used at a moment's notice whenever they are called for. The value of knowing the right thing to say to the right type of seller at the right time cannot be underestimated. It is the quality of what you say to sellers as well as how you say it that determines whether your business will go from 0 to 60 in record time or whether it will stall by the side of the highway leaving you stuck without a ride. A comprehensive system of scripts that tells you exactly what to say and how to say it when talking to sellers can cut years off your learning curve and add volume to your bottom line.

Here is an example of a script that I personally created and use to prescreen sellers and ascertain whether or not they are motivated.

Pre-screen Sellers Script

Seller Says: Hi, I'm calling you because I received a letter from you saying that you are interested in buying my house.

Me: Hello my name is Omar and yes I do buy houses may I have your name please? (Seller gives name)

Me: Hi (the person's name), what is the best phone number to reach you at? (Seller gives telephone number)

Me: Ok got it. (the person's name),what is the best time to call you? (Seller gives that time)

Me: May I have your email address if you have one? (Seller gives their email address)

Me: Can you tell me a little bit about the house? (Seller describes the house)

Me: What is the property's address? (Seller gives the address)

Me: What is the asking price of your house? (Seller gives the price)

Me: How did you arrive at your price? (Seller explains)

Me: What is the estimated value of your house? (Seller gives the answer)

Me: Your reason for selling it? (Seller gives motivation for selling)

Me: Does your house need repairs? (Seller gives the answer)

Me: If yes how much? (Seller gives the answer)

Me: Is your house listed? (Seller gives the answer)

(I was satisfied with the numbers that the seller gave me so I move on to the following)

Me: Ok thanks, let me explain to you exactly what we do at Dependable Home Buyers. We are real estate investors and we work with sellers like yourself to come up with creative solutions to buy your house at a fair price. I say at a fair price because we are not trying to steal your house but keep in mind that we are real estate investors and we are in this to make a profit. Do you have any problems with that?

(The Seller didn't have a problem so I asked the next set of pre-screening questions)

Me: Ok I need to ask you a few more questions to see if your house qualifies. Is that ok? (Seller says it's ok)

Me: What is the 1st Mortgage Balance? (Seller gives the answer)

Me: What is the 1st mortgage int. rate? (Seller gives the answer)

Me: What is the 1st Mortgage Monthly Payment? (Seller gives the answer)

Me: Does this include PI or PITI? (Seller gives the answer)

Me: 2nd Mortgage Balance? (Seller gives the answer)

Me: 2nd Mortgage int. rate? (Seller gives the answer)

Me: 2nd Mortgage Monthly Payment? (Seller gives the answer)

Me: Does this include PI or PITI (Seller gives the answer)

Me: Are Your Payments Current? (Seller gives the answer)

Me: If No how much behind? (Seller gives the answer)

Me: Would you sell your house for what you owe on it? (If Seller answers yes they are really motivated)

Me: Would you sell your house by allowing us to take over the payments? (If Seller answers yes they are really motivated)

Me: When do you want to move? (If Seller answers ASAP they are really motivated)

It is obvious how a script to pre-screen your sellers can be useful to you. To rewind back a little bit, in technique #8, I mentioned estate sales but what if you had to actually deal with an executor of an estate that's in probate as discussed in technique #29? Wouldn't it be nice to know exactly what to say to that executor under such unfortunate circumstances? Here's an example of a script that I normally follow when I communicate with an executor of an estate that's in probate.

What To Say To An Executor Of An Estate In Probate

Me: Hello my name is Omar Johnson can I speak to John Darling (the executor's name)?

Executor: This is John Darling speaking how may I help you?

Me: Hi John, first of all I would like to offer my condolences on your recent loss of your loved one. I know that this may be a difficult time for you and your family.

Executor: Thanks

Me: John, the purpose of my call today is to inform you about a valuable service that I have to offer that can be of great benefit to you during this difficult time period.

Executor: And what is that service Mr. Johnson?

Me: The services that I have to offer are I can buy real estate in most cases for all cash with a quick closing no matter what the area, price range or condition of the house. I buy properties in their "as is" condition with no contingencies which will result in a quick sale for the estate. In addition to buying real estate, I also purchase real estate contracts, notes, mortgages, automobiles, furniture, boats, jewelry or anything of value. Would that be of any interest to you?

If the executor answers yes to that question I then would ask them in the same polite manner --What items are they considering for sale? If these items appeal to me and I can get a substantial reduction in price, I would set up an appointment with the executor and close the deal. If the executor answers no to that question I would say to them – Ok I understand if anything changes can you give me a call?

I hope it is evident at this point the importance of using scripts in your dealings with sellers. You should have scripts at your disposal for every situation imaginable, but what if you presently don't? In that case I have the ultimate solution for you. I have a complete system of scripts that are available in my home study course "What To Say And How To Talk To Sellers In Your Real Estate Transactions" that covers all the possible situations and objections that you will encounter with sellers and how to appropriately respond to them. For more information just visit http://www.whattosaytoaseller.com.

Motivated Buyers

Now, let's look at the second part of the equation: **motivated buyers**. The second part of the equation which deals with finding and acquiring motivated buyers will make you rich if you master this process. Here's why, it's quite simple. Motivated buyers bring cash to the table. Therefore, the number one asset in your real-estate business are your buyers. So it is imperative that you know how to grow and create a killer buyers list and understand that your list should be tended to like a tree that sprouts money for leaves.

Creating Your Killer Buyers List

Here are some of the main reasons why you must have a killer buyers list in your arsenal:

- Selling properties are much easier when you have a list of active buyers ready to purchase your deals.

- A buyers list allows you to segregate your retail buyers from your wholesale buyers and your renters from your landlords. This is very important because when you add a property to your inventory you will know exactly what segment of your list to call to market that particular property.

- A buyers list will help you to determine where the greatest demand is in your town or city. This will allow you to focus your marketing dollars to locate motivated sellers in those specific areas.

- Having a killer buyers list will also enable you to maintain a continuous positive cash flow as long as you have properties in your inventory that are in demand.

- Having a well-stocked buyers list gives you a wider choice and enables you to pick and choose the best candidates for your properties.

- As you satisfy your customers from your buyers list, word will spread and you will establish a solid presence and reputation in the marketplace that will result in you growing your list by leaps and bounds.

Shockingly most aspiring real estate entrepreneurs don't have the slightest clue on how to create and grow a buyers list for their real estate business and as a result they suffer. Most of them are taught by real estate gurus to find the property first then run an ad in the newspaper to find buyers.

The problem with this approach is you better be able to find a buyer immediately or else you will be stuck with paying the holding cost of the property like utilities, the mortgage, taxes, insurance etc. until you find your actual buyer. I'm not too fond of this approach and neither should you be, because you are solely relying on luck and the timing of others. You are hoping that a buyer responds to your ad immediately or you will be facing a very unpleasant situation.

To ensure a quick sale, wouldn't it be much better for you to find your buyers first and then ask them what kind of properties they are looking for rather than finding a property first then looking for a buyer? The latter approach is loaded with too much uncertainty.

In fact, a lot of new investors I come across are full with the fear of the possibility of not selling a property that they have purchased creatively using such real estate investing strategies such as wholesaling, retailing, short sales, subject to, lease options and options, because they are afraid that they will be stuck with the property and would have to pay those aforementioned holding costs.

Unfortunately, these types of investors have put up psychological barriers based on those fears and they eventually and predictably pull back from aggressively pursuing properties. To be quite frank with you, I can understand their fears, because they are basing it on the actual fact of no matter how good of a deal you get on a property you plan to sell, a long holding selling period can eat away most or all of your profit.

Hopefully, you don't let this kind of fear consume you and destroy your chances of ever making money in real estate. To avoid this at all costs, you have to be able to know how to create and grow not just a buyers list, but a killer buyers list from scratch. You also must know how to specifically attract retail buyers as well as wholesale buyers.

The Two Types of Buyers In The Real Estate Market

Let me break that down for you. There are fundamentally two types of buyers in the real estate market. Those who buy to have a place to live and those who buy to make a profit. Buyers looking for a home are called retail buyers or home buyers. Buyers looking for a profit are called wholesale buyers or investors. Whether your business is geared towards wholesaling, retailing or combination of both, it is important for you to have a grasp on the mentality and buying habits of both types of buyers.

This is because if you are wholesaling, then your investor buyers will be selling to retail buyers at the end of the line. So, you must understand retail buyers in order to know how investors work. And if you are selling to retail buyers then you are an investor yourself and it would obviously behoove you to know as much as possible about the buying habits of investors.

One big difference between retail buyers and wholesale buyers are the types of properties they buy. Retail buyers are usually looking for a nice home to live in so their candidate properties are pretty, well maintained and updated, price near market value and in nice looking neighborhoods.

Wholesale buyers on the other hand want profitable investments. So, they are usually looking for property that they can acquire for below market value and improve and or rental property that is already occupied by a tenant. In this way, the types of deals you look for will be targeted to your audience or buyers.

Another key difference between retail buyers and wholesale buyers is in buying frequency. Wholesale buyers are buying as part of an ongoing business venture and those tend to buy repeatedly and your goal of course is to have them buy repeatedly from you.

In contrast, retail buyers typically have just one purchase to make, so they are very selective about the house they settle on and probably won't make another purchase for a long time once they have bought the home that they want to live in. This means if you are selling to wholesale buyers, you can run your business off a relatively small, steady list of consistent buyers, but if you are trying to sell to retail buyers then your buyers list not only needs to be bigger to compensate for the pickiness of the buyers, it also needs to be fed more to replace those who are constantly dropping off the market.

Thus for wholesaling, a tight, solid call of long-term regular buyers will carry you through where as for retailing you need a broad net of buyers that are constantly being replaced. Recognizing this difference is essential to designing your marketing plan for your real-estate business.

A buyers list is a living, growing organism, and as such needs to be cultivated and grown, more so than built. There are two parts to this equation, the first one being adding buyers to the list. Whether you are selling wholesale or retail, the bigger the list you have the more effective you will be at selling your properties, so in any event you should be continually adding names to your list for as long as you are doing business.

Prospecting And Marketing: Adding Buyers To Your List

There are two fundamental ways of adding buyers to your list: you can either seek them out and contact them (prospecting), or you can attract them to contact you (marketing). So, which is better? Trick question: neither is. You should be doing both prospecting and marketing at all times. The two processes will then support and reinforce each other.

Through prospecting you reach out to people who may not have heard of or contacted you otherwise and help to establish your presence within the business community. Yet through marketing you can give many more people an opportunity to hear your message and contact you.

Without prospecting to keep you in touch with what your clients want, your marketing can go stale. But without marketing to attract high volumes of business, your stream of potential clients can dry up quickly.

Prospecting is particularly important for contacting wholesale buyers, as many of them can be found and contacted through their advertising. The following is a short list of some of the ways you can find contact information for investors in your market:

− Browse classified ads in newspapers, local publications, and on classified ad websites. You will find many investors advertising in these places.

− Capture your prospects' contact information in the field. As you are driving neighborhoods be on the lookout for "we buy houses" bandit signs and other signals of investment activity, such as homes for rent or in the process of being rehabbed.

− Network in person by attending seminars, REI clubs, and other places where investors might congregate (such as property auctions). Be gregarious, meet as many people as you can, and don't be stingy with the business cards. Make it your goal to come away with as many new contacts as possible. Shyness is understandable, especially when you are unfamiliar, but if you go to a meeting like this and only watch and listen without introducing yourself to anybody, you are cheating yourself.

– On the Internet, join investor forums and chat rooms such as biggerpockets.com, activerain.com, Iwannanetwork.com, magicbullets.com and participate in the discussions. Join wholesaling websites such as rehablist.com which are designed to put wholesalers and investors in touch. Create profiles on business and personal networking sites and seek out other real estate professionals working in your market.

Just like in person, be gregarious, but don't worry about making all of your connections at once; rather, focus on being consistent over time. Each day leave a few comments on other peoples' profiles or blog posts and add a few new connections to your profile.

– Collect lists of houses for rent and contact the landlords. A landlord is, by definition, at least a one-time investor! These are some of the best leads because they potentially turn into buyers OR sellers.

Marketing is especially important for attracting large numbers of retail buyers, but it should be part of your strategy for attracting wholesale buyers as well. Here are just a few of the ways to get your marketing message to your prospects:

Classified Ads

Run your own classified ads, in local papers, publications, and online classified ad websites, advertising that you have houses for sale. This shouldn't be your main marketing strategy, but it shouldn't be neglected either.

If you are running classified ads either offline or online you can use the following two ads to attract retail buyers and wholesale buyers respectively. To attract wholesale buyers your ad would read:

Handyman Super Special

Cheap, Cash

222-2222

Here's an ad that you can use to attract lease purchase and owner financing prospects:

Lease Purchase & Owner Financed Homes Available

We have nice 3 and 4 bedroom homes available on owner financing or lease purchase programs. Call (800) 555-5555 to hear our 24hr prerecorded message or visit www.yourwebsite.com

To continue with the ways in which you can get your message out to potential motivated buyer prospects.

– Advertise on the Internet with your own website. Just be sure you create a marketing plan for driving traffic to it. If you don't presently have your own website to attract buyers I offer motivated buyer website templates. Just visit http://www.realestatewebsitestogo.info

– For wholesale buyers, run ads for your properties in online real estate forums and wholesaling sites.

– Keep track of every buyer who contacts you. If you are advertising a house for sale, add every buyer who calls you about that house to your permanent buyer list, even if they don't end up buying the house (which, obviously, most of them won't).

Strengthening Your Buyers List

If adding buyers to your list is one half of the growth equation, the other half is strengthening the ties with your existing prospects and buyers. It's not just the number of contacts you have that is important but also the relationships and reputation that you have with them. This reputation is built mainly by communication.

You should be staying in touch with your buyers on a regular basis by whatever means they prefer, whether by phone, email, or some other method. And the best thing to be communicating about is houses that you have for sale. The more quality, relevant, ACTIONABLE info you share with your buyers the better reputation you will have with them.

Also, as you get to know your buyers and they get to know you, you will build the confidence and familiarity that leads to sales. Furthermore, the more business people see you doing the more they will want to do business with you. Therefore you should always be working your list and never let it sit idle.

It's been said, "It's not what you know, it's who you know", but this still isn't quite true; the truth is, "It isn't who you know, it's who knows you". How much does it mean if you know Donald Trump? How much does it mean if Donald Trump knows you? Case closed.

How well do you know your buyers? More importantly, how well do your buyers know you? Do they know who you are and what you do?

Do they know what your distinguishing features and unique benefits are? Do they know how you do business? Do they owe you a favor? The better your buyers know you and the more highly they think of you, the more closely you will be linked in their minds with the service that you provide.

Let's not underestimate the importance of knowing your buyers, however. The better you know them as individuals the more special they will feel, and the more effectively you will be able to satisfy their needs.

You should certainly know as much as possible about their financial situation and the type of house they are looking for, as well as their business practices if they are an investor. Beyond this it helps to know about their personality, interests, and home life. The more intimate you are with your buyers the better you will be able to understand their motivations and the more ways you will be able to find to relate to them and thus help them.

Being intimate in your relationship with someone just means being real, being able to talk as friends and peers with no barriers to communication. This is exactly the kind of relationship you want to have with your most important clients.

So we have established that the more buyers you have on your list the better, and also that the more information you have related to each buyer the better as well. This indicates that you will need to have ready access to a large amount of information, and therefore an organized filing system is called for, ideally some sort of computer database or spreadsheet software.

There are several technological solutions to handle this situation, including storing the information either online or on your computer using contact manager or spreadsheet software. But if you have a website it might work out even better to include within it a form page to capture this information from buyers who visit the website and automatically enter it into a web database.

Regardless of the exact method used, your system should be functional enough to store all of the data you need while allowing for quick and easy access to view and modify it.

The information that you need to capture from each buyer will vary but at the very least it should include contact information, including fax and email, information about the type of property they are seeking, and information about their state of financing.

As mentioned before, the more relevant details you can add the better, but the information doesn't have to be gathered all at once up front. You should make it a point to stay in touch with your buyers regularly, and one way to do this is to call periodically and capture new pieces of information.

For example, you might say something in each conversation like "Hi Bob, this is Joe the wholesaler. I was calling to see what types of properties you are actively looking for. Are you interested in multi-family properties? I've got a great deal right now on some duplexes and triplexes."

This is especially relevant for wholesale buyers, who may not want to share too many details of their business with you until they get to know you better. Keep in mind that some people will want to be contacted less than others, so you should exercise judgment with this process, and also be sure that you have some good news or good information to offer when you make the contact.

A strong buyers list is obviously not created overnight, but requires cultivation over time, much like a garden. It becomes stronger the more you use it, the longer your buyers have known you and the more deals you have done with them.

Eventually it will even be able to practically run your business by itself. In the early stages it must be well tended and well fed, but with time and persistence it will build the momentum that will carry your business forward to increasing profitability and success.

What To Say To Your Buyers: 3 Stages of The Buying Process

Okay, I've already stressed the importance of knowing what to say and how to talk to sellers in your real-estate transactions to close deals. But also equally important is knowing what to say to your buyers. That's just plain common sense.

When selling real-estate creatively the sales process with your buyers will involve several different stages and it is imperative that you know how to communicate with your buyers during each and every stage.

For example, stage one will most likely involve you crafting a message or central theme that is designed to attract potential buyers. Once you have created your message, the next step in stage one would be to deliver that message through the various mediums such as classified ads, fliers, direct mail, etc. with the purpose of eliciting a response from potential buyer prospects who will be inquiring about the house that you have to sell or the special home ownership programs that you are offering if any.

So the bottom line is, you must know exactly what to say in your message to your potential buyer prospects in stage one because this will effectively lead to stage two of the sales process. In stage two, your buyer prospects will be calling you to find out more information on the houses that you are offering for sale. In this stage, you will be answering their questions, conveying the benefits of the properties that you are offering, and pre-screening them to weed out the prospects from the suspects.

Also in this particular stage, your prospects will be posing objections to you that you must be able to provide answers to and overcome. Therefore, in stage two, you must know exactly what to say to your buyer prospects in order to pre-screen them, convey the benefits, respond to their objections and to answer any questions that they might have. When you have effectively communicated with your prospects in stage two and they are seriously interested in buying the properties that you have to offer, this will allow you to navigate to stage three of the sales process.

Stage three. In stage three, you are on the verge of closing the sale. You will be hit with additional objections and it is critical that you are prepared to answer them because when you do answer them it will allow you to immediately go to the close. And once you've arrived at that point, all you have to do is know what to say to your buyer to close the deal because if you know what to say to them, it will result in you receiving a deposit, a down payment or flat out cash for the houses that you are selling.

But what if you don't know what to say to buyers? Quite frankly, if you don't know what to say to your buyers, you are dead in the water, because how are you ever going to make money from real estate? How would you be able to navigate and guide buyers through the aforementioned three stages of the sales process? Come on, let's get serious. You wouldn't be able to.

In order to succeed at any type of sales and especially in real-estate where you are asking people to part with large sums of money, you have to be totally prepared. I mean, you already know your buyers will ask questions, so shouldn't you anticipate beforehand the typical questions that they are going to ask you and have your responses ready to answer them?

The same principle applies to objections. You know that they are going to come up and most of them are typical, so shouldn't you already know beforehand how you will respond and handle those objections? You are probably wondering how in the heck are you going to be able to know and remember beforehand all of the different questions and objections that will be posed to you and the appropriate responses for the various buyers that you will be encountering.

If you have designed your real-estate business to obtain maximum profits, you will be selling to retail buyers as well as wholesale buyers. Some of the questions that you would ask these two types of buyers in order to pre-screen them will be similar and dissimilar in nature.

Same thing goes for the objections and your responses to those objections for wholesale buyers versus retail buyers. They will also be both similar and dissimilar in nature. In addition, your wholesale buyers and retail buyers will be further segmented based on what type of creative financing you are making available to them to purchase your properties.

For example, you may allow your retail buyers to purchase their homes creatively through a lease purchase or owner finance situation where there is no qualifying at the bank or you might allow them to acquire a home through some sort of work for equity program. I know that this seems like a lot to digest, but it's really not if you systemize the entire process by using a comprehensive set of scripts that enables you to know exactly what to say to your buyers to sell your houses and inventory fast.

In fact, here are some of the reasons why you should have a bona fide script system in place when dealing with your buyers.

- Having a set of scripts will enable you to know what to say to your buyers and when to say it.

- By sticking to a script you avoid being tongue tied and losing control of the conversation as well as the negotiations with your buyers.

- By utilizing scripts there should be no more mumbling, stumbling and fumbling of your words because of practice and rehearsal.

- Scripts allow you to hire and train people to sell your houses for you enabling your business to run on auto-pilot.

- By employing scripts on a consistent and continuous basis when communicating with your buyers you will become a master closer, which will result in you making a ton of cash.

So in essence everything I've discussed in this book deals with marketing because as I mentioned to you earlier real estate marketing is the business and if your real-estate business is not where you want it to be, the problem more than likely lies in your marketing. It is either non-existent, shame on you or just plain vanilla ordinary.

In fact, I want you to always remember the following three principles. Principle number one: the strength of your bottom line in your real-estate business is proportional to the strength of your marketing. Period. Principle number two: being a marketing expert is significantly more important than being a creative real-estate expert. Principle number three: **Motivated Sellers + Motivated Buyers = $**

In conclusion, if you don't have a full fledge comprehensive script system to know what to say to buyers I offer one in my home study course entitled "What To Say To Buyers To Sell Houses Fast" For more information just visit: http://www.whattosaytobuyers.com. I also offer a comprehensive real estate coaching program. For more information just visit

http://www.theultimaterealestatecoach.com

A perfect complement to this book is another real estate book that I authored entitled Creative Real Estate Investing Strategies And Tips.

Good Luck and Much Success,

Omar Johnson

www.ingramcontent.com/pod-product-compliance
Lightning Source LLC
Chambersburg PA
CBHW071237170526
45165CB00003B/1134